POWER ENGLISH

BASIC LANGUAGE SKILLS FOR ADULTS

7

Dorothy Rubin

TRENTON STATE COLLEGE

CAMBRIDGE Adult Education
Prentice Hall Regents, Englewood Cliffs, NJ 07632

PHOTO CREDITS

CHAPTER ONE: Charles Gatewood
CHAPTER TWO: © 1982 Rick Maiman, PANS
CHAPTER THREE: American Cancer Society
CHAPTER FIVE: National Archives

Editorial supervision: Timothy Foote
Production supervision: Alan Gold
Manufacturing buyer: Mike Woerner
Photo editor: Page Poore

© 1990 by Prentice Hall Regents
Published by Prentice-Hall, Inc.
A Division of Simon & Schuster
Englewood Cliffs, New Jersey 07632

Printed in the United States of America

10 9 8 7 6 5 4 3 2 1

ISBN 013–688508–X

Prentice-Hall International (UK) Limited, *London*
Prentice-Hall of Australia Pty. Limited, *Sydney*
Prentice-Hall Canada Inc., *Toronto*
Prentice-Hall Hispanoamericana, S.A., *Mexico*
Prentice-Hall of India Private Limited, *New Delhi*
Prentice-Hall of Japan, Inc., *Tokyo*
Simon & Schuster Asia Pte. Ltd., *Singapore*
Editora Prentice-Hall do Brasil, Ltda., *Rio de Janeiro*

CONTENTS

Power English: Basic Language Skills for Adults is a ten-book series dedicated to helping adults at the ABE level develop their skills in usage, sentence structure, mechanics, and composition. *Power English* consists of the locator test for the series, eight text/workbooks, and a series review book.

There are five chapters in each of the text/workbooks. The several lessons in each chapter cover a variety of writing skills. The comprehensive Chapter Reviews and Posttests in each book provide skill reinforcement. To facilitate diagnosis, there are Progress Charts for recording students' Chapter Review and Posttest performance. Answers are in a special section at the end of each book. The section can be left in the book so that students can check their own work, or since its pages are perforated, it can be removed.

Power English is comfortable for an adult whose reading level is between 4.0 and 8.0. Each lesson is a simple and concise presentation of a specific writing skill. In the instructional portion of a lesson, under the heading **Read the following** students study examples of a specific writing skill at work. Under **Did you notice?** they read short, clear explanations of the skill at hand. Because a typical lesson reinforces and expands upon skills taught in earlier lessons, a section called **Do you remember?** reviews pertinent rules and concepts previously presented. The **Try it out** portion of a lesson provides exercise for applying and practicing the new and reviewed skills.

Power English encourages the rapid and enjoyable acquisition of fundamental writing skills. The program is based on sound learning principles and is devised to keep the student actively engaged throughout. It incorporates the following:

- self-pacing
- graduated levels of difficulty
- distributed practice
- immediate feedback
- overlearning
- teaching of generalizations where applicable
- selections based on adult interests

Power English is founded on the principle of overlearning, which fosters enduring retention of information and skills. Overlearning occurs when students continue practicing a skill even after they think they have learned it. In every chapter and book in the *Power English* series, through a variety of formats, students exercise skills they have learned in previous chapters and books.

The structure of the *Power English* series makes it versatile. It can be used in conventional classroom settings, in tutorial situations and clinics, or by students who work independently.

CHAPTER ONE

CAPITALIZING (NAMES OF MAGAZINES)

Read the following:	Better Homes and Gardens Sports Illustrated Playboy Women's Day
Did you notice?	Most words in the names of magazines begin with capital letters. Magazine names are underlined.
Do you remember?	Most words in the titles of books begin with capital letters.

Try it out.   Write each sentence over correctly.

1. sally and i love to read ladies home companion on saturdays.

_____

_____

2. Pedro just finished reading mark twain's tom sawyer.

_____

_____

3. the last wednesday in february, bonnie, cheryl, and i are going to chicago.

_____

_____

4. jim and i love the pictures in national geographic.

_____

_____

5. fortune is a magazine about our nation's business.

_____

_____

6. us news and world report is an interesting magazine.

_____

_____

GO ON TO THE NEXT PAGE

7. on february 11 i am traveling to china to learn chinese.

_____

_____

8. president ortez of benson college asked senator brown to give the opening address in spanish.

_____

_____

9. on mother's day we are sending our mother to france.

_____

_____

10. my favorite magazine is <u>popular mechanics</u>.

_____

_____

STOP CHECK ANSWERS ON PAGE 137.

SINGULAR AND PLURAL SUBJECTS

Read the following:

Craig is driving to Atlanta.
The children's room is messy.
They are buying a new bedroom set.
Housing and food cost more and more each year.

Did you notice?

The underlined words in the above sentences are the nouns and pronouns in the complete subject that control the verbs.

There is at least one noun or pronoun in the complete subject of a sentence.

When the noun or pronoun in a complete subject names one thing, the subject of the sentence is singular.

When the noun or pronoun in a complete subject names more than one thing, the subject of the sentence is plural.

When there are two or more nouns or pronouns in a complete subject, the subject of the sentence is plural.

Do you remember?

Nouns that show possession do not control verbs.

Try it out.

Underline the nouns and pronouns that control the verbs in each of the following sentences. Write **S** in the blank if the subject of the sentence is singular. Write **P** in the blank if the subject of the sentence is plural.

1. Bob and I need more time. _____

2. We know all about that. _____

3. It is not true. _____

4. Miss Hansen works for me. _____

5. Someone should know who she is. _____

6. Everyone wants to go out with him. _____

7. The mice are eating the cheese. _____

8. This day is one to remember. _____

9. Everybody should help us. _____

10. The Matoses' present is not here. _____

STOP CHECK ANSWERS ON PAGE 137.

RECOGNIZING SENTENCES

Read the following:	There is a check (√) by each of the sentences. √ Don't go there. No one has. Here we say.
Did you notice?	**No one has** and **Here we say** are not sentences. Both have subjects and verbs, but neither expresses a complete thought.
Do you remember?	A sentence has two parts, a complete subject and a predicate. A sentence expresses a complete thought; it makes sense.

Try it out. Put a check (√) by each of the sentences.

☐ **1.** Please hold the door for us.

☐ **2.** The men are going to be here soon.

☐ **3.** Run fast.

☐ **4.** Drop that here.

☐ **5.** When he arrives there.

☐ **6.** Hold onto that.

☐ **7.** They are.

☐ **8.** After the ride home.

☐ **9.** My little old cat has.

☐ **10.** Who told you that?

STOP CHECK ANSWERS ON PAGE 137.

SENTENCE PARTS

Read the following:	These are not sentences; they are sentence parts.
	While I stay here.
	Before we go.
	Until she left.
Now read this:	These sentences include the parts from the list above.
	<u>While I stay here</u>, you can go out.
	We should close the windows <u>before we go</u>.
	<u>Until she left</u>, I felt uncomfortable.
Did you notice?	The sentence parts have subjects and verbs.
	However, they do not express complete thoughts.
	They can each be part of a longer sentence.

Try it out. Here are some sentence parts and some sentences. Underline each of the sentence parts. Put a check (√) by each of the sentences.

☐ 1. Even though I am not going.

☐ 2. Did you send him here?

☐ 3. Who is there?

☐ 4. Before Carl does anything.

☐ 5. How much is that?

☐ 6. Stop doing that.

☐ 7. When we were there.

☐ 8. Where they are going.

☐ 9. Until you say that.

☐ 10. Since that took place.

STOP CHECK ANSWERS ON PAGE 137.

COMBINING SENTENCES

| **Try it out.** | Write one sentence that combines the two in each of the following pairs. Follow the model above. |

1. I am thinking of quitting my job.
   My husband wants a change also.

   _____

   _____

2. We are not getting ahead here.
   It is hard making ends meet.

   _____

   _____

3. Our children like it here.
   My parents live close to us.

   _____

   _____

4. My parents want us to stay.
   Our friends are upset about our leaving.

   _____

   _____

5. We probably won't do anything.
   My husband and I will remain here.

   _____

   _____

STOP   CHECK ANSWERS ON PAGE 137.

DIRECT QUOTATIONS

Read the following:	Julio said, "I enjoy my work." Flores said, "I like my work, too."
Do you remember?	A direct quotation gives the exact words of a speaker. A comma (,) goes after the word **said**. Quotation marks (" ") go around the speaker's words. The first word of a direct quotation is capitalized.

Try it out.   Write these direct quotations correctly.

1. Sachiko said please help me fix this.

   _____

2. Donna said I need more help.

   _____

3. José said Steve and I are going to the party.

   _____

4. Miss Eng said please give the child her coat.

   _____

5. Maria said this is very heavy.

   _____

6. Bob said last year was a hard one for me.

   _____

7. Paolo said no, I will not go.

   _____

8. Mr. Darbari said call Joe and tell him to meet us.

   _____

9. Jennifer said my friends are visiting me soon.

   _____

10. Leila said it is fun being a judge.

   _____

STOP   CHECK ANSWERS ON PAGE 137.

END MARKS (PUNCTUATION MARKS)

Read the following:
They are darling children.
What do you want?
She is a wonderful person!
Go now.

Do you remember?
A statement ends with a period (.).
A question ends with a question mark (?).
A sentence that shows strong feeling ends with an exclamation point (!).
A command usually ends with a period (.).
If a command shows strong feeling, it ends with an exclamation point (!).
A command usually has the unstated subject: **you.**
End marks can also be called **end punctuation**.

Try it out.   Put the proper end mark at the end of each sentence.

1. Which person said that

2. How terrible that is

3. Clara and Daniella are going to a show

4. Please turn that around

5. Hold that person

6. How do you feel today

7. Try to behave yourself

8. What a wonderful day this is

9. I never asked him anything

10. Will you be here tomorrow

STOP   CHECK ANSWERS ON PAGE 137.

ADJECTIVES AND LINKING VERBS

Read the following:
Ken seems <u>younger</u> than he.
She is <u>thinner</u> than I.
His wife looks <u>pretty</u> today.
This smells <u>fresh</u>.
I feel <u>well</u>.

Did you notice?
The words **younger**, **thinner**, **pretty**, **fresh**, and **well** are adjectives.
In each sentence, the adjective describes the noun or pronoun in the complete subject.

Do you remember?
Describing words that tell about the subject can come after verbs, such as **seems**, **is**, **looks**, **smells**, and **feel**.

Try it out. Fill in each blank in the sentences with an adjective from the list. Use each adjective **only once**.

ADJECTIVE LIST

best	brighter	fresher	happier	happiest
shiniest	softer	taller	terrible	well

1. The moon looks _____ tonight than last night.

2. Do you feel _____ today?

3. She sounds _____ today than yesterday.

4. These flowers smell _____ than those.

5. Her eyes are the _____ I have ever seen them.

6. The roast tastes the _____ a few days later.

7. Bob is _____ than Dan, the basketball player.

8. The room smelled _____ after the flood.

9. This is the _____ day in my life.

10. Those chairs look _____ than the ones I have.

STOP CHECK THE ANSWERS ON PAGE 137.

REGULAR AND IRREGULAR VERBS

Read the following:

TIME	REGULAR VERB	IRREGULAR VERB
Present	Fred worries.	Fred grows.
Past	Fred worried.	Fred grew.
Future	Fred will worry.	Fred will grow.
Right now	Fred is worrying.	Fred is growing.
Up to now	Fred has worried.	Fred has grown.

Do you remember? Regular verbs end with **d** or **ed** in past time and with **has** and **have**.

Irregular verbs have special forms for past time and with **has** and **have**.

There is no difference in the ways regular and irregular verbs show present or future time or action right now.

Try it out. Write two forms for each verb: the form for past and the form for up to now (with **has**).

	REGULAR VERBS				IRREGULAR VERBS	
	PAST	UP TO NOW			PAST	UP TO NOW
1. work	_____	_____		6. run	_____	_____
2. chase	_____	_____		7. catch	_____	_____
3. play	_____	_____		8. know	_____	_____
4. cry	_____	_____		9. drink	_____	_____
5. dress	_____	_____		10. take	_____	_____

STOP CHECK ANSWERS ON PAGE 137.

11

THE VERB *BE*

Read the following: Jim <u>is</u> very happy today.
They <u>are</u> not leaving yet.
My father <u>was</u> the head of his company.
They <u>were</u> not here yesterday.
She <u>has been</u> here for ten years.
They <u>have been</u> there for hours.

Do you remember? There are several forms of the verb **be**.
These are some of the forms:

TIME	FORM OF **BE**
Present	am, are, is
Past	was, were
Future	will be
From before to now	has been, have been

Try it out. Fill in each blank with one of the forms of **be** from the above list.

1. Andrew _____ at my house two weeks ago.

2. I _____ very happy here now.

3. When we saw him, we _____ upset.

4. They _____ at my house now.

5. This _____ a good day for me so far.

6. Henri and his friends _____ here in two hours.

7. Someone _____ here a few times already.

8. That child _____ ill now.

9. We _____ here at least once before.

10. I _____ at the factory yesterday.

STOP CHECK ANSWERS ON PAGE 138.

THE VERBS *SPEAK, SPEAKS, SPOKE, WILL SPEAK, HAS SPOKEN, HAVE SPOKEN,* AND *HAD SPOKEN*

Read the following:

Sharon <u>speaks</u> well.   Seth and Sharon <u>speak</u> well.
He <u>spoke</u> well.   They <u>spoke</u> well.
I <u>will speak</u>.   We <u>will speak</u>.
She <u>has spoken</u>.   They <u>have spoken</u>.
He <u>had spoken</u>.   They <u>had spoken</u>.

Did you notice?

The verbs **speaks** and **speak** describe action in the present.
Speak goes with plural nouns and the pronouns I, **you**, **we**, and **they**.
Speaks goes with singular nouns and the pronouns **he**, **she**, and it.
The word **spoke** describes action in the past.
The words **will speak** describe action in the future.
Spoken goes with the helping verbs **has**, **have**, and **had**.

Try it out.   Fill in each blank with the correct form of the verb **speak**.

1. We _____ to them very often.

2. Mario and I had _____ to them before.

3. I _____ to you later.

4. His friend _____ too loudly all the time.

5. She had _____ about that.

6. John _____ to me just before.

7. Gary and I have _____ often about you.

8. They _____ to their boss tomorrow.

9. Mary has _____ about that a few times.

10. Hiro and Noriko _____ very highly of you yesterday.

STOP   CHECK ANSWERS ON PAGE 138.

THE WORDS *A* AND *AN*

Try it out.   Put **a** or **an** before each of the following.

1. _____ idea

2. _____ big ape

3. _____ older child

4. _____ tired man

5. _____ oak

6. _____ pet

7. _____ island

8. _____ onion

9. _____ bicycle

10. _____ handsome man

11. _____ oil well

12. _____ half-hour

13. _____ even line

14. _____ young man

15. _____ house

16. _____ uncle

17. _____ actor

18. _____ yard

19. _____ Easter egg

20. _____ x-ray

STOP   CHECK ANSWERS ON PAGE 138.

WRITING AN INVITATION

Read the following:

March 4, 1990

Dear Terry and Marcia,

Arthur and I are having a housewarming party at 7:00 P.M. on March 20 at our new apartment. It is an informal dinner party, so dress comfortably.

Our new address is 61 Main Street, and our new phone number is (212) 555-7643.

Please phone by March 16 to let us know if you can make it. We are looking forward to seeing you.

Fondly,

Miriam and Arthur

Do you remember?
An invitation tells the following.
- Who is having the party
- Where the party will be
- What kind of party it is
- The day, date, and time of the party

GO ON TO THE NEXT PAGE

Try it out. Fill in this form to invite someone to a housewarming party.

SPELLING

Read the following:
We will do that <u>only</u> for you.
I've done it <u>once</u> already.
What is your <u>name</u>?
She is my <u>cousin</u>.
We are going on a <u>picnic</u>.

Did you know?
The underlined words in the sentences above are often misspelled.

Try it out.
Look at each word. Then cover it and write it in the blank. Check your spelling. Finally, write a sentence using the word.

1. only   _____

_____

2. once   _____

_____

3. name   _____

_____

4. cousin   _____

_____

5. picnic   _____

_____

STOP CHECK SAMPLE ANSWERS ON PAGE 138.

CAPITALIZING (NAMES OF MAGAZINES)
Write each sentence over correctly.

1. alice and i enjoy reading reader's digest and tv guide.

   _____

2. Frank and Ted read do it yourself and the complete handyman.

   _____

3. chuck and i get sports magazine and the fisherman's guide.

   _____

4. gale and sally read romance magazines, such as true story.

   _____

5. i like to read movie magazines, such as hollywood magazine.

   _____

SINGULAR AND PLURAL SUBJECTS
Underline the nouns and pronouns in the subjects of the following sentences. Write **S** in the blank if the subject of the sentence is singular. Write **P** in the blank if the subject of the sentence is plural.

1. Blanca Silva and her friends read about sad love affairs. _____

2. The love affairs always begin happy and then end sad. _____

3. The story usually begins with a nice boy meeting a nice girl. _____

4. Then it ends in some death or tragedy. _____

5. I do not like to read such sad stories. _____

RECOGNIZING SENTENCES
Put a check (√) by each of the sentences.

☐ 1. When she arrives.

☐ 2. Until this day is over.

☐ 3. Stop running so fast.

☐ 4. Is that the truth?

☐ 5. Robert and I are.

GO ON TO THE NEXT PAGE

SENTENCE PARTS

Here are some sentence parts and some sentences. Underline each of the sentence parts. Put a check (√) by each of the sentences.

☐ **1.** When they go there.

☐ **2.** Help is on the way.

☐ **3.** After we saw them.

☐ **4.** Anyone can do that.

☐ **5.** Until we arrive.

COMBINING SENTENCES

Write one sentence that combines the two in each of the following pairs. Use the word **and** in the combination.

1. The tall trees look like soldiers.
   The flowers look like pretty young girls.

_____

_____

2. Hank was too tired to play.
   His partner was not feeling well.

_____

_____

3. We studied hard for the test.
   It was worth it.

_____

_____

4. George and Donna have a new home.
   They just bought a new car and boat.

_____

_____

5. I would like to change jobs.
   My boyfriend would like to move to another town.

_____

_____

GO ON TO THE NEXT PAGE

DIRECT QUOTATIONS

Write these direct quotations correctly.

1. Sidney said i need another helper.

   _____

2. Pina said that is not too strong.

   _____

3. Ali said i am visiting my family shortly.

   _____

4. Florence said my family is visiting me soon.

   _____

5. Teresa said these are enough supplies for the week.

   _____

END MARKS (PUNCTUATION MARKS)

Put the proper end mark at the end of each sentence.

1. Where are we going

2. Do you know the way

3. This is the wrong road

4. This is ridiculous

5. Stop this minute

ADJECTIVES AND LINKING VERBS

Fill in each blank in the sentences with an adjective from the list. Use each adjective **only once**.

ADJECTIVE LIST

beautiful   better   cheerful   sadder   worst

1. I'm sorry to hear that you are _____ than you were yesterday.

2. The trees, grass, and leaves look _____ this time of the year.

3. I'm glad your family feels _____ today.

4. The birds sound _____ today.

5. This dump smells the _____ it ever has.

GO ON TO THE NEXT PAGE

REGULAR AND IRREGULAR VERBS

Write two forms for each verb: the form for the past and the form for up to now (with **has**).

	PAST	UP TO NOW
1. go	_____	_____
2. catch	_____	_____
3. forget	_____	_____
4. eat	_____	_____
5. try	_____	_____

THE VERB *BE*

Fill in each blank with the correct form of the verb *be*.

1. It _____ a great day so far.

2. My family _____ at the library before.

3. We _____ having a nice time now.

4. Everybody _____ at the picnic yesterday.

5. They _____ ready for an hour.

THE VERBS *SPEAK, SPEAKS, SPOKE, WILL SPEAK, HAS SPOKEN, HAVE SPOKEN,* AND *HAD SPOKEN*

Fill in each blank with the correct form of the verb *speak*.

1. Sharon _____ to her mother all the time now.

2. They _____ several times already.

3. I _____ to her tomorrow.

4. He had _____ about you often.

5. I _____ to my boss about you yesterday.

THE WORDS *A* AND *AN*

Put **a** or **an** before each of the following.

1. _____ orange

2. _____ oatmeal cracker

3. _____ closet

4. _____ boat

5. _____ ad

6. _____ show

7. _____ hole

8. _____ hammer

9. _____ ounce

10. _____ enemy

GO ON TO THE NEXT PAGE

WRITING AN INVITATION

Write a letter to invite someone to a party to celebrate a new job.

_____

_____

_____

_____

_____

_____

_____

_____

_____

_____

SPELLING

Use each of the following words in a sentence.

1. only

_____

2. once

_____

3. name

_____

4. cousin

_____

5. picnic

_____

STOP   CHECK ANSWERS BEGINNING ON PAGE 138.

Count how many items you answered correctly in each **Section** of the Chapter One Review. Write your score per section in the **My Scores** column. If all of your section scores are as high as the **Good Scores**, go on to Chapter Two. If any of your section scores are lower than the **Good Scores**, study the lessons on the assigned **Review Pages** again before you go on to Chapter Two.

Section	Good Scores	My Scores	Review Pages
Capitalizing (Names of Magazines)	4 or 5		2–3
Singular and Plural Subjects	4 or 5		4
Recognizing Sentences	4 or 5		5
Sentence Parts	4 or 5		6
Combining Sentences	4 or 5		7
Direct Quotations	4 or 5		8
End Marks (Punctuation Marks)	4 or 5		9
Adjectives and Linking Verbs	4 or 5		10
Regular and Irregular Verbs	4 or 5		11
The Verb **Be**	4 or 5		12
The Verbs **Speak, Speaks, Spoke, Will Speak, Has Spoken, Have Spoken**, and **Had Spoken**	4 or 5		13
The Words **A** and **An**	8, 9, or 10		14
Writing an Invitation	A correct letter		15–16
Spelling	4 or 5		17

CHAPTER TWO

CAPITALIZING (NAMES OF PLACES)

Read the following:	East Berlin West Virginia I live in the North. I am going south.
Do you remember?	The words **east**, **west**, **north**, and **south** are capitalized when they are part of a name. They are also capitalized when they name a location. They are not capitalized when they indicate a direction.

Try it out.   Write each sentence over correctly.

1. jim and phyllis are traveling east.

_____

2. pauline and i are going to the east to see the statue of liberty.

_____

3. the franklin bank is in north carolina.

_____

4. Ron traveled north, and then he went to the south.

_____

5. next may mehdi and i are moving west to california.

_____

6. diego juarez and his wife are going to the east soon.

_____

7. mrs. peters lives in the east and travels south often.

_____

8. the russo family is going west to south dakota.

_____

9. who was the president when the north and the south entered the civil war?

_____

10. in january we are going to the west and then to the north.

_____

STOP   CHECK ANSWERS ON PAGE 139.

COMBINING SENTENCES

Read the following:	My brother works very hard. He never seems to have any money.
Now read this:	My brother works very hard, but he never seems to have any money.
Did you notice?	The subjects and predicates of the two sentences are different. The two short sentences are combined in the long sentence. A comma (,) and the word **but** are used to combine the sentence. The combination does not shorten the sentences.
Do you remember?	The word **but** shows a contrast between two ideas.

Try it out.   Write one sentence that combines the two in each of the following pairs. Follow the above model.

1. Jane is going to stop soon.
   She has not finished yet.

   _____

2. I want to get married soon.
   My girlfriend wants to wait.

   _____

3. We have a number of problems.
   I feel we can work them out.

   _____

4. She wants to wait to have children.
   I want them soon.

   _____

5. My sister thinks I won't marry Gloria.
   My friends think I will.

   _____

STOP   CHECK ANSWERS ON PAGE 139.

SHORTENING SENTENCES

Read the following:	My father and my mother and my sister are here. My friend Jack and my friend Ben and my friend Joe are going hunting.
Now read this:	My father, mother, and sister are here. My friends Jack, Ben, and Joe are going hunting.
Did you notice?	In each sentence there are three phrases in a list. The word **my** is used only once in each shortened sentence. The word **friend** in the second longer sentence is changed to **friends** in the shortened sentence.
Do you remember?	Commas (,) can be used to shorten sentences with three or more words or phrases in a list. The comma replaces **and**—except for the last **and**—in the list. There is no comma after the last word or phrase in the list.

Try it out.	Shorten the following sentences by using commas.

1. He has his coffee and his toast and his cereal every morning.

_____

_____

2. I gave her my new dress and my new sweater and my new pearls to wear.

_____

_____

3. My friend Bob and my friend Gary and my friend Terry are coming to my house.

_____

_____

4. My old car and my old bike and my old typewriter fell apart at the same time.

_____

_____

5. In the movie the wild foxes and the wild wolves and the wild dogs ran together.

_____

_____

STOP CHECK ANSWERS ON PAGE 139.

SENTENCE PARTS

Read the following: These are not sentence parts:
When I arrived.
After the game is over.
Although she is here now.

Did you notice? The sentence parts have subjects and verbs.
However, they do not express complete thoughts.

Do you remember? A sentence part can be part of a longer sentence.

Try it out. Here are some sentence parts and some sentences. Underline each of the sentence parts. Put a check (√) by each of the sentences.

☐ **1.** Although she is happy now.

☐ **2.** In a moment the game will be over.

☐ **3.** When she spoke.

☐ **4.** Until you decide.

☐ **5.** Who is that person?

☐ **6.** While we were there.

☐ **7.** Help is on the way.

☐ **8.** Run to the store for me.

☐ **9.** Which one she liked.

☐ **10.** Don't hold onto her.

STOP CHECK ANSWERS ON PAGE 139.

SENTENCE PARTS (INDEPENDENT AND DEPENDENT WORD GROUPS)

Try it out. Underline the dependent word group in each of the following sentences.

1. Although she was not feeling well, she went to the party.

2. We were upset when they showed it to us.

3. Before they saw us, they were ready to leave.

4. We talked about our problems while we were at Angela's house.

5. When you return, we will go the movies.

6. I wanted some praise after I worked so hard.

7. Although he is nice, I can't vote for him.

8. I will not change my mind unless they change theirs.

9. Since it is too late to do anything now, I will not go.

10. Even though she is happy here, she wants to quit.

STOP CHECK ANSWERS ON PAGE 140.

DIRECT QUOTATIONS

Read the following:	Mike said, "Thank you for your help." Robin asked, "Why did you go there?"
Do you remember?	A direct quotation gives the exact words of a speaker. The quotation can be a statement or a question. A comma (,) goes after the word **said** or **asked**. Quotation marks (" ") go around the speaker's words. The first word of a direct quotation is capitalized. The period (.) or question mark (**?**) at the end of a quotation is inside the quotation marks.

Try it out.   Write these direct quotations correctly. Add the correct end mark.

1. Keung asked who told you that lie

_____

2. Hank asked what do you want

_____

3. Marie said I need more time to think

_____

4. Kim said the car is not broken

_____

5. Carlos asked will you come to see me soon

_____

6. Tran asked do you like little animals

_____

7. Michel said I enjoy traveling

_____

8. Jerry asked will I have time to do that

_____

9. Hideo said there is nobody left who can do it

_____

10. Emilia said let's have a party on New Year's Eve

_____

STOP   CHECK ANSWERS ON PAGE 140.

DIRECT AND INDIRECT QUOTATIONS

Read the following:	Paco said that he can't go with Jaime tomorrow.
Now read this:	Paco said, "I can't go with Jaime tomorrow."
Did you notice?	An indirect quotation can be changed to a direct quotation. An indirect quotation tells what the speaker said but does not use the speaker's words. There is no special punctuation in an indirect quotation. A direct quotation gives the exact words of the speaker. Quotation marks are used.

Try it out. The following sentences contain indirect quotations. Write each sentence over so that it contains a direct quotation.

1. She said that this is the happiest day of her life.

_____

2. Mito said that he wants to visit us tomorrow.

_____

3. Helen said that she told Jack to buy the car.

_____

4. Choi said that she wants to teach school next year.

_____

5. Ted said that he is going on vacation tomorrow.

_____

6. Flores said that the mail has not arrived yet.

_____

7. She said that she does not need any help.

_____

8. Dick said that the car door is stuck.

_____

GO ON TO THE NEXT PAGE

9. Betty said that her boss is giving her a raise.

_____

10. Henry said that he will ask his boss for a raise.

_____

STOP   CHECK ANSWERS ON PAGE 140.

PRONOUNS

Read the following:

	COMPLETE SUBJECT	PREDICATE
	I	like her.
	She	hit me.
	We	saw them.

Do you remember? The pronouns **I**, **he**, **she**, **we**, and **they** are used as subjects of sentences.

The pronouns **me**, **him**, **her**, **us**, and **them** are used in predicates.

The pronouns **you** and **it** are used both as subjects and in predicates.

| **Try it out.** | Fill in each blank with the correct pronoun.

1. _____ saw _____. (**me** and **she**)

2. Fred and _____ need _____. (**them** and **I**)

3. _____ helped _____. (**we** and **them**)

4. _____ called _____. (**us** and **they**)

5. _____ hit _____. (**us** and **they**)

6. _____ scared _____. (**it** and **us**)

7. _____ read _____. (**it** and **we**)

8. _____ sees _____. (**us** and **she**)

9. Sharon and _____ know _____. (**them** and **I**)

10. Dave and _____ saw _____. (**us** and **she**)

STOP CHECK THE ANSWERS ON PAGE 140.

MORE THAN ONE (PLURAL)

Read the following:

one cake	two cakes
one box	two boxes
one church	two churches
one pass	two passes
one shelf	two shelves
one child	two children
one sheep	two sheep
one spy	two spies

Do you remember?

These are some of the ways to make a noun plural:

If it ends with **ch**, **s**, **sh**, **ss**, or **x**, add **es**.

If it ends with **f** or **fe**, change the ending to **ve** and add **s**.

If it ends with a consonant + **y**, change the **y** to **i** and add **es**.

There are no rules to follow to form the plurals of some nouns. You must memorize plurals like **children** and **sheep**.

Try it out.   Write the plural form of each of the following nouns.

1. car _____
2. elf _____
3. lash _____
4. woman _____
5. mouse _____
6. crash _____
7. Charles _____

8. kiss _____
9. fly _____
10. lunch _____
11. wife _____
12. fox _____
13. face _____
14. tooth _____

15. bed _____
16. mess _____
17. witch _____
18. candy _____
19. day _____
20. baby _____

STOP   CHECK ANSWERS ON PAGE 140.

THE VERBS *STEAL, STEALS, STOLE, WILL STEAL, HAS STOLEN, HAVE STOLEN,* AND *HAD STOLEN*

Read the following:

Alan steals.
He stole something.
I will steal.
She has stolen.
He had stolen.

Alan and Jane steal.
They stole something.
We will steal.
They have stolen.
They had stolen.

Did you notice?

The verbs **steals** and **steal** describe action in the present.
Steal goes with plural nouns and the pronouns **I**, **you**, **we**, and **they**.
Steals goes with singular nouns and the pronouns **he, she,** and **it**.
The word **stole** describes action in the past.
The words **will steal** describe action in the future.
Stolen goes with the helping verbs **has, have,** and **had**.

Try it out.   Fill in each blank with the correct form of the verb **steal**.

1. They have _____ many things over the years.

2. Jorge and I never have _____ anything.

3. Donald _____ a book from the store yesterday.

4. My friend had _____ things before he was a teenager.

5. Colette _____ apples from the fruit stand before.

6. Someone _____ my car last week.

7. Did you _____ that?

8. She had _____ the truck.

9. He has _____ toys.

10. Cats _____ food from the garbage cans every day.

STOP   CHECK ANSWERS ON PAGE 140.

ADVERBS

Try it out. In each blank, write the comparing form of the adverb correctly.

1. His friend did _____ on the test than you. (**well**)

2. My girlfriend did the _____ of all. (**well**)

3. At the picnic it rained the _____ I have ever seen. (**heavy**)

4. Rodolfo speaks _____ than Miguel. (**rapidly**)

5. Sang and I drove _____ by the park than on the highway. (**slowly**)

6. Peter laughed the _____ when he saw how we were dressed. (**hard**)

7. My friends drive _____ than I do. (**fast**)

8. The child held the rope the _____. (**tight**)

9. Flores writes _____ than you. (**often**)

10. Sara screamed _____ this time than last time. (**loud**)

STOP CHECK ANSWERS ON PAGE 140.

SHOWING OWNERSHIP OR BELONGING TO (POSSESSION)

Read the following:	This book's cover is nice. These books' covers are nice. The spy's name is Mr. X. The spies' names are Mr. X and Ms. Y. The man's face is burned. The men's faces are burned.
Did you notice?	In the first sentence in each pair, the underlined word shows singular ownership. In the second, the underlined words shows plural ownership.
Do you remember?	For singular nouns, possession is shown with this mark (') + **s**. When a plural noun ends with **s**, possession is shown by adding this mark (') after the **s**. Some plural nouns, like **men**, do not end in **s**. For such plural nouns, ownership is shown by adding this mark (') + **s**.

Try it out.	For each of the following nouns, write the form that shows ownership.

1. goose _____
2. woman _____
3. wives _____
4. game _____
5. couch _____

6. shelves _____
7. candy _____
8. task _____
9. hostess _____
10. tomato _____

STOP CHECK ANSWERS ON PAGE 140.

CONTRACTIONS

Read the following:

I have	I've
you have	you've
he has	he's
she is	she's
it is	it's
we are	we're

Do you remember? The pronouns **I**, **you**, **he**, **she**, **it**, **we**, and **they** can be joined with **am**, **are**, **is**, **has**, or **have**.

When a pronoun is joined with **am**, **are**, or **is**, the first letter of the verb is replaced by this mark (').

When a pronoun is joined with **has** or **have**, the **ha** in the verb is replaced by this mark (').

Try it out.	Write the contraction for each of the following.

1. she has _____

2. we have _____

3. I have _____

4. they have _____

5. you are _____

6. we are _____

7. I am _____

8. they are _____

9. she has _____

10. it is _____

STOP   CHECK ANSWERS ON PAGE 140.

SPELLING

Read the following:

I hate to say good-bye to people.
Are you going there again?
I will see you in a week.
That pink is a pretty color.
I like the color blue.

Did you know?

The underlined words in the sentences above are often misspelled.

Try it out.

Look at each word. Then cover it and write it in the blank. Check your spelling. Finally, write a sentence using the word.

1. good-bye _____

_____

2. again _____

_____

3. week _____

_____

4. color _____

_____

5. blue _____

_____

STOP CHECK SAMPLE ANSWERS ON PAGE 140.

40

CAPITALIZING (NAMES OF PLACES)

Write each sentence over correctly.

1. aunt lisa and i live in north dakota and like to travel east.

   _____

2. jim, ted, and josé are going to the south on vacation.

   _____

3. my uncle mike has traveled to the west and all over.

   _____

4. our club is taking a bus trip to the east this summer.

   _____

5. i live in west virginia and travel to south carolina often.

   _____

COMBINING SENTENCES

Write one sentence that combines the two in each of the following pairs. Use the word **but** in the combination.

1. Marriage is a big step.
   I am ready for it.

   _____

   _____

2. My boyfriend wants us to live together first.
   My parents are very upset about this.

   _____

   _____

3. They do not want me to move in with my boyfriend.
   I do not want to lose him.

   _____

   _____

GO ON TO THE NEXT PAGE

4. I really want to get married and raise a family.
   I can't convince my boyfriend to do this.

   _____

   _____

5. I may move in with my boyfriend.
   It's not what I really want to do.

SHORTENING SENTENCES

Shorten the following sentences by using commas.

1. My friend Mary and my friend Kim and my friend Sue are here.

   _____

   _____

2. The hot roll and the hot bacon and the hot eggs are delicious.

   _____

   _____

3. My pal Jack and my pal Herbert and my pal Artie and my pal Julio and I are going hunting next week.

   _____

   _____

4. Kenji's old couch and old chair and old table need to be repaired.

   _____

   _____

5. I love my dog and my cat and my pet canary.

   _____

   _____

SENTENCE PARTS

Here are some sentence parts and some sentences. Underline each of the sentence parts. Put a check (√) by each of the sentences.

☐ 1. When Jane leaves.

☐ 2. Until I can be on my own.

☐ 3. Please go there with me.

☐ 4. After the game is over.

☐ 5. This is very funny.

GO ON TO THE NEXT PAGE

SENTENCE PARTS (INDEPENDENT AND DEPENDENT WORD GROUPS)

Underline the dependent word group in each of the following sentences.

1. When Doris came to the party, she looked very upset.

2. She left suddenly after she had been there a short while.

3. While we were talking about this, we heard some noise outside.

4. We didn't pay too much attention to it since it was very noisy inside.

5. When we left, we saw Doris lying face down in the street.

DIRECT QUOTATIONS

Write these direct quotations correctly. Add the correct end mark.

1. Julio said this year is going to be our best one

2. Peter asked who could be so stupid

3. George asked why are they taking so long

4. Martin said I refuse to pay so much for this

5. Yuriko said that man just stole something from the store

DIRECT AND INDIRECT QUOTATIONS

The following sentences contain indirect quotations. Write each sentence over so that it contains a direct quotation.

1. Gloria said that the roads are very slippery today.

2. Sally said that the bus is running late today.

3. Antoine said that his car has a flat tire.

4. Paul said that he needs a ride home from work.

5. Maria said that she has more work to do.

GO ON TO THE NEXT PAGE

PRONOUNS

Fill in each blank with the correct pronoun.

1. Sharon and _____ saw _____. (**him** and **I**)

2. The twins and _____ know _____. (**them** and **I**)

3. _____ loves _____. (**him** and **she**)

4. _____ helped _____. (**they** are **us**)

5. _____ saved _____. (**him** and **we**)

MORE THAN ONE (PLURAL)

Write the plural form of each of the following nouns.

1. tire _____   5. wife _____   8. wolf _____

2. body _____   6. child _____   9. roof _____

3. box _____   7. knife _____   10. building _____

4. scarf _____

THE VERBS *STEAL, STEALS, STOLE, WILL STEAL, HAS STOLEN,* *HAVE STOLEN,* AND *HAD STOLEN*

Fill in each blank with the correct form of the verb **steal**.

1. Judy and her brother _____ money from me yesterday.

2. They have _____ before.

3. Some people _____ anything and everything.

4. My friend had _____ a car before.

5. He still _____ things now.

ADVERBS

In each blank, write the comparing form of the adverb correctly.

1. Diane works the _____ of anyone. (**hard**)

2. She did _____ on the test than she expected. (**poorly**)

3. I work _____ than you. (**hard**)

4. The ambulance driver drove the _____ of anyone I have ever seen. (**carelessly**)

5. Everyone acted _____ at the party than at work. (**friendly**)

GO ON TO THE NEXT PAGE

SHOWING OWNERSHIP OR BELONGING TO (POSSESSION)

For each of the following nouns, write the form that shows ownership.

1. wolf _____
2. ladies _____
3. tool _____
4. James _____

5. children _____
6. toy _____
7. sales _____

8. box _____
9. fire _____
10. men _____

CONTRACTIONS

Write the contractions for each of the following.

1. I have _____
2. they have _____
3. he has _____
4. they are _____

5. it has _____
6. we are _____
7. she is _____

8. you are _____
9. it is _____
10. you have _____

SPELLING

Use each of the following words in a sentence.

1. good-bye

_____

2. again

_____

3. week

_____

4. color

_____

5. blue

_____

STOP   CHECK ANSWERS BEGINNING ON PAGE 140.

Count how many items you answered correctly in each **Section** of the Chapter Two Review. Write your score per section in the **My Scores** column. If all of your section scores are as high as the **Good Scores**, go on to Chapter Three. If any of your section scores are lower than the **Good Scores**, study the lessons on the assigned **Review Pages** again before you go on to Chapter Three.

Section	Good Scores	My Scores	Review Pages
Capitalizing (Names of Places)	4 or 5		26
Combining Sentences	4 or 5		27
Shortening Sentences	4 or 5		28
Sentence Parts	4 or 5		29
Sentence Parts (Independent and Dependent Word Groups)	4 or 5		30
Direct Quotations	4 or 5		31
Direct and Indirect Quotations	4 or 5		32–33
Pronouns	4 or 5		34
More Than One (Plural)	8, 9, or 10		35
The Verbs **Steal, Steals, Stole, Will Steal, Has Stolen, Have Stolen,** and **Had Stolen**	4 or 5		36
Adverbs	4 or 5		37
Showing Ownership or Belonging To (Possession)	8, 9, or 10		38
Contractions	8, 9, or 10		39
Spelling	4 or 5		40

CHAPTER THREE

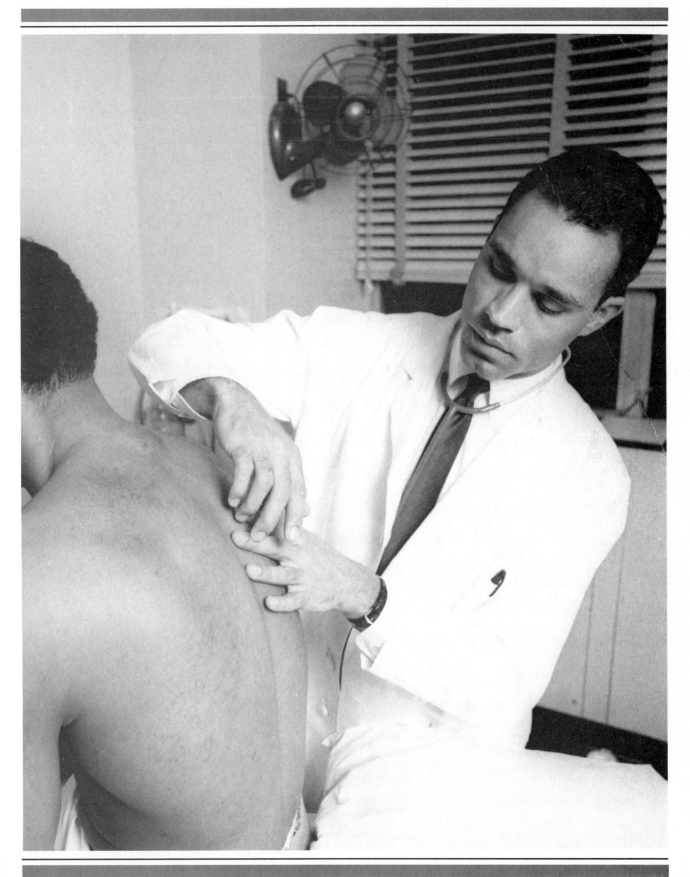

CAPITALIZING (COMMON NOUNS AND PROPER NOUNS)

Read the following:

COMMON NOUNS	PROPER NOUNS
street	Drake Street
city	New York City
state	Florida
country	England
day	Monday
month	February
holiday	Christmas
company	General Electric Company

Do you remember? A common noun names a type of person, place, or thing. Common nouns are not capitalized.

A proper noun names a specific person, place, or thing. Proper nouns are capitalized.

Try it out. Here is a list of nouns. Correct any nouns that are not written correctly. Put a **C** in the blank by those that are correct.

1. mexico _____
2. james _____
3. avenue _____
4. abc company _____
5. spring _____
6. tuesday _____
7. chicago _____
8. poetry _____
9. columbus day _____
10. father's day _____
11. hotel _____
12. arithmetic _____
13. carol _____
14. ohio _____
15. week _____
16. Year _____
17. world war II _____
18. italy _____
19. jeff _____
20. judge Brown _____

STOP CHECK ANSWERS ON PAGE 142.

COMBINING SENTENCES

Read the following:	I like Gerardo. He likes me. He treats me well. I don't treat him so well. Be nicer to him. He will leave you.
Now read this:	I like Gerardo, and he likes me. He treats me well, but I don't treat him so well. Be nicer to him, or he will leave you.
Did you notice?	Each pair of short sentences is combined with a comma (,) and the word **or**, **but**, or **and**.
Do you remember?	The use of **or**, **but**, or **and** depends on sentence meaning.

Try it out. Write one sentence that combines the two in each of the following pairs. Use a comma with **or**, **but**, or **and** in the sentence you write.

1. My brother fell in love with a beautiful girl.
   She does not love him.

   _____

   _____

2. He walks around with a long face all the time.
   It is difficult to cheer him up.

   _____

   _____

3. I am trying to get them together.
   It is probably a lost cause.

   _____

   _____

4. My brother needs to meet someone else.
   He will become even more depressed.

   _____

   _____

GO ON TO THE NEXT PAGE

5. We have to do something soon.
   My brother will wind up in the hospital.

   _____

   _____

STOP   CHECK ANSWERS ON PAGE 142.

COMBINING SENTENCES

Try it out.   Write one sentence that combines the two in each of the following pairs. Use a comma with **or**, **but**, or **and** in the sentence you write.

1. Go to the doctor today for a check-up.
You may have a problem later on.

_____

_____

2. Gregory needs to see a lawyer.
You also need advice.

_____

_____

3. This may work fine.
I am not too sure.

_____

_____

4. Mr. and Mrs. Knott are checking out today.
Their friends are staying another day.

_____

_____

GO ON TO THE NEXT PAGE

5. Do you want to stay here another day?
Do we need to go home?

_____

_____

STOP   CHECK ANSWERS ON PAGE 142.

SENTENCE PARTS (INDEPENDENT AND DEPENDENT WORD GROUPS)

Read the following:

DEPENDENT WORD GROUPS

Before I come to your house.
Until she tells you the truth.

INDEPENDENT WORD GROUPS

I need to change my clothes.
I will not speak to her.

Now read this:

Before I come to your house, I need to change my clothes.
I will not speak to her until she tells you the truth.

Do you remember?

There are two kinds of word groups: **dependent** and **independent**. Dependent word groups are not sentences; they are sentence parts. Independent word groups are sentences.
A dependent word group can be combined with an independent word group to make a longer sentence.
A comma (,) separates the two word groups when the dependent group comes first.

Try it out.   Underline the dependent word group in each of the following sentences.

1. They should not go there when it is dark.

2. Although I like my work, I don't want to do anything now.

3. After we saw them, we knew they were in trouble.

4. I was very tired after I worked so hard.

5. Even though she practices hard, she doesn't play too well.

6. When the storm started, we were on the road.

7. I am going there because I love him.

8. Sara will meet you there unless she changes her mind.

9. Come back to my house when the show is over.

10. Unless you want trouble, try to help them.

STOP   CHECK ANSWERS ON PAGE 142.

COMBINING INDEPENDENT AND DEPENDENT WORD GROUPS

| **Try it out.** | Find the dependent word group that goes with each independent word group to form a sentence that makes sense. Write the letter in the blank. |

INDEPENDENT WORD GROUPS

_____ 1. Herb found his door open

_____ 2. Sharon went to the game

_____ 3. It is no fun to go out

_____ 4. We are waiting

_____ 5. I hold that against her

_____ 6. The police arrived at my home

_____ 7. Giorgio practices the piano every day

_____ 8. My car will not move

_____ 9. Matsue and Junko have done a lot

_____ 10. The ballplayers are not happy

DEPENDENT WORD GROUPS

a. because she loves football.

b. until his fingers are tired.

c. because it is out of gas.

d. since they left school.

e. when he came home.

f. until Hossein arrives.

g. if you have no pals.

h. because she hurt my friend.

i. because they lost the game.

j. after the crook had left.

STOP   CHECK THE ANSWERS ON PAGE 142.

THE PRONOUNS *ANYBODY, ANYONE, EVERYBODY, EVERYONE, NOBODY, NO ONE, SOMEBODY,* AND *SOMEONE*

Read the following:	<u>Anybody</u> can do that. <u>Everybody</u> is present. <u>Nobody</u> has it. <u>Somebody</u> is here.	<u>Anyone</u> can do that. <u>Everyone</u> is present. <u>No one</u> has it. <u>Someone</u> is here.
Do you remember?	The underlined words in the above sentences are pronouns. They can stand for any person. They are singular and go with singular verbs, such as **is** and **has**.	

Try it out.   Underline the verb that is correct for the sentence.

1. Nobody (**is** or **are**) in the room.

2. (**Has** or **Have**) anybody seen him?

3. Someone here (**has** or **have**) done it.

4. Nobody (**do** or **does**) that better than you.

5. Anybody (**know** or **knows**) that.

6. Nobody (**help** or **helps**) them.

7. Someone (**was** or **were**) not telling the truth.

8. Nobody (**read** or **reads**) the ads.

9. Anyone (**has** or **have**) the right to stay here.

10. Everyone (**work** or **works**) in town.

STOP   CHECK ANSWERS ON PAGE 142.

THE VERBS *WRITE, WRITES, WROTE, WILL WRITE, HAS WRITTEN, HAVE WRITTEN,* AND *HAD WRITTEN*

Read the following:

Carla <u>writes</u> often.   Carla and Ana <u>write</u> often.
She <u>wrote</u> often.   They <u>wrote</u> often.
I <u>will write</u>.   We <u>will write</u>.
She <u>has written</u>.   They <u>have written</u>.
He <u>had written</u>.   They <u>had written</u>.

Did you notice?

The verbs **writes** and **write** describe action in the present.
Write goes with plural nouns and the pronouns **I**, **you**, **we**, and **they**.
Writes goes with singular nouns and the pronouns **he**, **she**, and **it**.
The word **wrote** describes action in the past.
The words **will write** describe action in the future.
Written goes with the helping verbs **has**, **have**, and **had**.

Try it out.   Fill in each blank with the correct form of the verb **write**.

1. Vencente _____ me a letter last week.

2. Akemi and I _____ to each other often.

3. He had _____ about that.

4. My wife _____ to me when I go away.

5. We have _____ to her a number of times.

6. Lan _____ very well when she was a child.

7. She has _____ a good book.

8. Luiz _____ to his mother yesterday.

9. Claude had _____ me a funny letter.

10. She _____ to us later.

STOP   CHECK ANSWERS ON PAGE 142.

SHOWING OWNERSHIP OR BELONGING TO (POSSESSION)

Read the following:	Fred's house was on fire. The girls' faces were red. Charles's mother is my friend. The children's school is near.
Do you remember?	For singular nouns, possession is shown with this mark (') + **s**. When a plural noun ends with **s**, possession is shown by adding this mark (') after the **s**. Some plural nouns, such as **children**, do not end in **s**. For such plural nouns, ownership is shown by adding this mark (') + **s**.

Try it out. The nouns that show ownership in these sentences are written incorrectly. Find each of those nouns and write their correct forms in the blanks.

1. His cars radio is broken.   _____

2. Jennifers eyes are blue.   _____

3. The geeses' eggs are missing.   _____

4. His wifes' car is here.   _____

5. That thiefs' name is Sam.   _____

6. I need one owners book.   _____

7. The childrens' toys are here.   _____

8. Victors' hand is hurt.   _____

9. Giselles' gloves are in the closet.   _____

10. The churchs door is broken.   _____

STOP   CHECK ANSWERS ON PAGE 142.

THE COMMA (SETTING OFF WORDS)

Read the following: Of course, it's a good idea.
However, I'm not sure.
She wanted more money, of course.
He, however, did not want to lend it.

Did you notice? Phrases or words like **of course** and **however** are set off (separated) from the rest of a sentence by a comma or commas.
If the phrase or word comes at the beginning of a sentence, a comma goes after it.
If it comes at the end, a comma goes before it.
If it comes in the middle, commas go before and after it.

Now read this: Here are some other phrases and words that are usually set off by commas:

also	furthermore	nevertheless
besides	indeed	perhaps
for example	moreover	therefore

Try it out. Insert commas where they are needed in the following sentences to set off phrases or words.

1. Moreover I have a lot of time to do it.

2. Indeed that is a good idea.

3. She said however that she would stay with us.

4. We felt moreover that we could make a lot of money that way.

5. She saw however that it wouldn't work.

6. Therefore I need more time to stay here.

7. He does look silly indeed.

8. Furthermore anyone who says anything will be in trouble.

9. We learned for example that it would be dangerous to do that.

10. You can perhaps think of another way to do it.

STOP CHECK ANSWERS ON PAGE 142.

ABBREVIATIONS (SHORTENED WORDS)

Read the following: A list of words and their abbreviations follows.

WORD	ABBREVIATION	WORD	ABBREVIATION
Afternoon	P.M.	Doctor	Dr.
Avenue	Ave.	Drive	Dr.
Before noon	A.M.	Reverend	Rev.
Boulevard	Blvd.	Road	Rd.
Company	Co.	Street	St.

Did you notice? Abbreviations are short forms for words.
They usually are made up of letters from the words they abbreviate.
When a word begins with a capital letter, its abbreviation does, too.
A period (.) is placed at the end of an abbreviation.

Try it out. Fill in each blank with the correct abbreviation.

1. Carol will meet us on Spruce _____ tomorrow (**Boulevard**)

2. It is 10:00 _____, and he is still asleep. (**before noon**)

3. The King _____ sells good clothes. (**Company**)

4. _____ John Stone lives on Bank _____ near the church. (**Reverend; Street**)

5. At 6:00 _____ we listen to the news. (**afternoon**)

6. We read about _____ Barnes in the newspaper. (**Reverend**)

7. Rick lives on Hardy _____ and works at the Dugan Clothing _____ near there. (**Drive; Company**)

8. Rodrico and Marie went to _____ Johnson's office on Hale _____ this morning. (**Doctor; Avenue**)

9. The Dale _____ just hired a new president. (**Company**)

10. Please send that to Marsh _____ tomorrow. (**Drive**)

STOP CHECK ANSWERS ON PAGE 143.

WRITING A BUSINESS LETTER

Read the following: Here is a business letter.

213 Hardy Drive
Atlanta, Georgia 30320
December 15, 1990

Angela Rosas
ABC Publishing Company
2100 Madison Avenue
New York, New York 10017

Dear Ms. Rosas:

   Your company has been sending me magazines that I did not order. Please tell your people to stop sending them to me.
   I will not pay for something I do not want and did not order. Moreover, I do not want to go to the expense and bother of returning magazines that I did not order.

Sincerely yours,

Lisa King

GO ON TO THE NEXT PAGE

Follow the example on page 60. Write a business letter to the **president** of the **XYZ Tool Company** to complain that you did not get the set of tools you ordered. The company's address is **791 Moore Street, New York, New York 10003**. (You do not know the company president's name.)

STOP CHECK SAMPLE LETTER ON PAGE 143.

SPELLING

Read the following:
I have done more work <u>since</u> Tuesday.
Did you <u>receive</u> my gift.
I am happy <u>because</u> you are here.
She has a bad <u>cough</u>.
Please give me another <u>piece</u> of cake.

Did you know?
The underlined words in the sentences above are often misspelled.

| **Try it out.** | Look at each word. Then cover it and write it in the blank. Check your spelling. Finally, write a sentence using the word. |

1. since   _____

_____

2. receive   _____

_____

3. because   _____

_____

4. cough   _____

_____

5. piece   _____

_____

STOP CHECK SAMPLE ANSWERS ON PAGE 143.

ALPHABETIZING (USING THE DICTIONARY)

Do you remember? A dictionary has guide words at the top of each page. The guide words tell which are the first and last words on that page.
All words between the two guide words are on that page in alphabetical order.

Read the following: Here is a sample of the guide words at the top of a dictionary page.

plant	please

Try it out. Use the guide words **plant** and **please** to answer these questions. Write **Yes** or **No** in each blank.

1. Is the word **plan** on this page? _____

2. Is the word **plate** on this page? _____

3. Is the word **plum** on this page? _____

4. Is the word **pluck** on this page? _____

5. Is the word **plow** on this page? _____

6. Is the word **plot** on this page? _____

7. Is the word **plane** on this page? _____

8. Is the word **place** on this page? _____

9. Is the word **plier** on this page? _____

10. Is the word **play** on this page? _____

STOP CHECK ANSWERS ON PAGE 143.

CAPITALIZING (COMMON NOUNS AND PROPER NOUNS)

Here is a list of nouns. Correct any nouns that are not written correctly. Put a C in the blank by those that are correct.

1. north carolina _____
2. miss brown _____
3. Holiday _____
4. summer _____
5. Stone company _____

6. new mexico _____
7. season _____
8. mother's day _____
9. robert _____
10. france _____

COMBINING SENTENCES

Write one sentence that combines the two in each of the following pairs. Use a comma with **or**, **but**, or **and** in the sentence you write.

1. You should help your parents more.
   Your brother should try to be nicer to them.

   _____

   _____

2. The phone rang.
   There was no one on the line.

   _____

   _____

3. The workers want a raise.
   They do not want to strike.

   _____

   _____

4. The workers need more money.
   Their company can't afford to give raises.

   _____

   _____

GO ON TO THE NEXT PAGE

5. Jack must fly to Chicago today.
He will lose his plane fare.

_____

_____

SENTENCE PARTS (INDEPENDENT AND DEPENDENT WORD GROUPS)

Underline the dependent word group in each of the following sentences.

1. After I left, someone robbed the store.

2. I am leaving when she arrives.

3. Unless you hear differently, I will meet you later.

4. I will help her because she needs my help.

5. I get a headache when she is here.

COMBINING INDEPENDENT AND DEPENDENT WORD GROUPS

Find the dependent word group that goes with each independent word group to form a sentence that makes sense. Write the letter in the blank.

INDEPENDENT WORD GROUP	DEPENDENT WORD GROUP
____ 1. Sue wants to be a designer	a. when she was in school.
____ 2. Art was her best subject	b. because he believes in them.
____ 3. Sue and her sister are going into business	c. until they can be on their own.
____ 4. Their brother is helping them raise money	d. after they save enough money.
____ 5. Their parents are helping	e. because she loves art.

THE PRONOUNS _ANYBODY, ANYONE, EVERYBODY, EVERYONE, NOBODY, NO ONE, SOMEBODY,_ AND _SOMEONE_

Underline the verb that is correct for the sentence.

1. Nobody (**want** or **wants**) to hire me now.

2. Everybody (**seems** or **seem**) to have a job except for me.

3. Somebody (**has** or **have**) to help me soon.

4. Everyone (**is** or **are**) too busy to help me.

5. (**Do** or **Does**) anyone know what I should do?

GO ON TO THE NEXT PAGE

THE VERBS *WRITE, WRITES, WROTE, WILL WRITE, HAS WRITTEN, HAVE WRITTEN,* AND *HAD WRITTEN*

Fill in each blank with the correct form of the verb **write**.

1. Raimundo _____ to his brother yesterday.

2. They _____ to each other all the time.

3. Yukio has _____ to his friend Sadahiro for years.

4. I _____ to my parents tomorrow.

5. Harold had _____ to me before.

SHOWING OWNERSHIP OR BELONGING TO (POSSESSION)

The nouns that show ownership in these sentences are written incorrectly. Find each of those nouns and write their correct forms in the blanks.

1. Rauls used car is not running.   _____

2. Alices' dress is too small for her.   _____

3. My cars key is lost.   _____

4. Our wive's club is having a party.   _____

5. The roses's stems are very long.   _____

THE COMMA (SETTING OFF WORDS)

Insert commas where needed in the following sentences to set off phrases or words.

1. Therefore I do not need to go.

2. Patricio said moreover that he would do it.

3. It is too dangerous however.

4. We should perhaps put it off.

5. Frank and Mike however want to do it now.

ABBREVIATIONS (SHORTENED WORDS)

Fill in each with the correct abbreviation.

1. Please meet _____ Franco Pelli on Fifth _____ later.
   (Reverend; Avenue)

2. I am going to _____ Huang's office on Perry _____ today.
   (Doctor; Street)

3. I work for the Dixon _____ on Kale _____ near here.
   (Company; Drive)

GO ON TO THE NEXT PAGE

4. _____ John Sanders will speak at 4:00 _____ today.
   (Reverend; afternoon)

5. The Soto Supply _____ on Morse _____ just fired people.
   (Company; Road)

WRITING A BUSINESS LETTER

Write a letter to the **president** of the **Empire Clothing Company**. Tell him or her that you were sent the wrong jacket. You do not know the president's name. The company's address is **368 Field Avenue, Tulsa, Oklahoma 74121**.

GO ON TO THE NEXT PAGE

67

SPELLING

Use each of the following words in a sentence.

1. since

_____

2. receive

_____

3. because

_____

4. cough

_____

5. piece

_____

ALPHABETIZING (USING THE DICTIONARY)

Use the guide words **wreck** and **wrote** to answer these questions. Write **Yes** or **No** in each blank.

1. Is the word **written** on this page? _____

2. Is the word **wrong** on this page? _____

3. Is the word **wreath** on this page? _____

4. Is the word **wrath** on this page? _____

5. Is the word **write** on this page? _____

STOP   CHECK ANSWERS BEGINNING ON PAGE 143.

Count how many items you answered correctly in each **Section** of the Chapter Three Review. Write your score per section in the **My Scores** column. If all of your section scores are as high as the **Good Scores**, go on to Chapter Four. If any of your section scores are lower than the **Good Scores**, study the lessons on the assigned **Review Pages** again before you go on to Chapter Four.

Section	Good Scores	My Scores	Review Pages
Capitalizing (Common Nouns and Proper Nouns)	8, 9, or 10		48
Combining Sentences	4 or 5		49–52
Sentence Parts (Independent and Dependent Word Groups)	4 or 5		53
Combining Independent and Dependent Word Groups	4 or 5		54
The Pronouns **Anybody, Anyone, Everybody, Everyone, Nobody, No One, Somebody,** and **Someone**	4 or 5		55
The Verbs **Write, Writes, Wrote, Will Write, Has Written, Have Written,** and **Had Written**	4 or 5		56
Showing Ownership or Belonging To (Possession)	4 or 5		57
The Comma (Setting off Words)	4 or 5		58
Abbreviations (Shortened Words)	4 or 5		59
Writing a Business Letter	A correct letter		60–61
Spelling	4 or 5		62
Alphabetizing (Using the Dictionary)	4 or 5		63

A Declaration by the Representatives of the UNITED STATES OF AMERICA, in General Congress assembled.

When in the course of human events it becomes necessary for one people to dissolve the political bands which have connected them with another, and to ~~advance from that subordination in which they have hitherto remained,~~ & to assume among the powers of the earth the separate and equal station to which the laws of nature & of nature's god entitle them, a decent respect to the opinions of mankind requires that they should declare the causes which impel them to the separation.

We hold these truths to be self-evident; that all men are created equal ~~& independent~~, that ~~from that equal creation they derive~~ they are endowed by their creator with ~~rights~~ inherent & inalienable, among ~~which~~ these are life, & liberty, & the pursuit of happiness; that to secure these rights, governments are instituted among men, deriving their just powers from the consent of the governed; that whenever any form of government ~~shall~~ becomes destructive of these ends, it is the right of the people to alter or to abolish it, & to institute new government, laying it's foundation on such principles & organising it's powers in such form, as to them shall seem most likely to effect their safety & happiness. prudence indeed will dictate that governments long established should not be changed for light & transient causes: and accordingly all experience hath shewn that mankind are more disposed to suffer while evils are sufferable, than to right themselves by abolishing the forms to which they are accustomed. but when a long train of abuses & usurpations [begun at a distinguished period, &] pursuing invariably the same object, evinces a design to ~~subject~~ reduce

CAPITALIZING (HISTORICAL PERIODS AND DOCUMENTS)

Try it out.   Write each sentence over correctly.

1. the american constitution is a very special document.

_____

_____

2. the american revolution had several causes.

_____

_____

3. the russian revolution took place after the american revolution.

_____

_____

4. the french revolution took place after the american revolution.

_____

_____

5. the bill of rights is part of the constitution.

_____

_____

6. in pauline's history class she learned about the roman empire.

_____

_____

GO ON TO THE NEXT PAGE

7. the industrial age in the united states saw the rise of cities.

_____

_____

8. in washington, d.c., i visited the lincoln memorial.

_____

_____

9. on veteran's day we honor those who fought for our country.

_____

_____

10. next march nina and i are visiting philadelphia to see the liberty bell.

_____

_____

STOP CHECK ANSWERS ON PAGE 144.

COMBINING SENTENCES

Read the following:	We should start soon. The work won't be finished on time. I am going skating. My sister is going to a movie. I cooked the food. He ate it.
Now read this:	We should start soon, <u>or</u> the work won't be finished on time. I am going skating, <u>but</u> my sister is going to a movie. I cooked the food, <u>and</u> he ate it.
Did you notice?	Each pair of short sentences is combined with a comma (,) and the word **or**, **but**, or **and**.
Do you remember?	The use of **or**, **but**, or **and** depends on sentence meaning.

Try it out.	Write one sentence that combines the two in each of the following pairs. Use a comma with **or**, **but**, or **and** in the sentence you write.

1. This is a terrible story.
   It must be told.

   _____

   _____

2. Jeff is a married man.
   He goes out with women.

   _____

   _____

3. One woman he went out with had AIDS.
   She gave the virus to Jeff.

   _____

   _____

4. Jeff did not know he had the virus.
   He would have avoided giving it to his wife.

   _____

   _____

GO ON TO THE NEXT PAGE

5. His wife was expecting a baby.
The baby was born with AIDS.

_____

_____

STOP CHECK ANSWERS ON PAGE 144.

SENTENCE PARTS (INDEPENDENT AND DEPENDENT WORD GROUPS)

Read the following:	Although she is your sister, I do not like her. We will go out for dinner after the game is over.
Did you notice?	The dependent word groups are underlined in the sentences above.
Do you remember?	There are two kinds of word groups: **dependent** and **independent**. Independent word groups are sentences. Dependent word groups are not sentences; they are sentence parts. A dependent word group can be combined with an independent word group to make a longer sentence. A comma (,) separates the two word groups when the dependent group comes first.

Try it out. Underline the dependent word group in each of the following sentences.

1. Although he feels sorry about it, it is too late.

2. People must be more careful because there are more dangers today.

3. Unless people protect themselves properly, they may have big problems.

4. Unfortunately, little children get hurt because some adults are careless.

5. It is very sad when a baby is born with AIDS.

6. It is something that should not have happened.

7. After people heard about it, they avoided him.

8. Now, his friends cross the street when they see him.

9. His poor wife cries when she visits her baby in the hospital.

10. This is a terrible tragedy because a whole family has been destroyed.

STOP CHECK ANSWERS ON PAGE 144.

END MARKS (PUNCTUATION MARKS)

Read the following:	Felipe asked what they were doing. What are you doing?
Did you notice?	The first sentence does not ask a question. Because it makes a statement, it ends with a period. The second sentence asks a question. It ends with a question mark.

Try it out. Here are ten sentences. Put the correct end mark at the end of each sentence.

1. Ben asked when they were leaving

2. Andres asked who was meeting them later

3. What kind of person would do that

4. Is she really that angry at us

5. Francis asked why they did that

6. Marianne asked how old she was

7. Did the police arrest anyone

8. What is her address

9. Nader asked whether the mail was due shortly

10. Everyone wondered what caused the accident

STOP CHECK ANSWERS ON PAGE 144.

PRONOUNS (SHOWING OWNERSHIP OR BELONGING TO)

Read the following:

This is <u>my</u> house.   It is <u>mine</u>.
This is <u>your</u> house.   It is <u>yours</u>.
This is <u>his</u> house.   It is <u>his</u>.
This is <u>her</u> house.   It is <u>hers</u>.
This is <u>its</u> house.   It is <u>its</u>.
This is <u>our</u> house.   It is <u>ours</u>.
This is <u>their</u> house. It is <u>theirs</u>.

Do you remember?   The pronouns **my**, **mine**, **your**, **yours**, **his**, **her**, **hers**, **its**, **our**, **ours**, **their**, and **theirs** show ownership.

| **Try it out.** | In each blank in the sentences, write a pronoun that shows ownership.

1. That is Augusto's name.

   That name is _____.

2. This is Carla's hat.

   This hat is _____.

   This is _____ hat.

3. This is Carlos's house.

   This house is _____.

   This is _____ house.

4. These are the children's chairs.

   These are _____.

   These are _____ chairs.

5. Maria's foot is swollen.

   _____ foot is swollen.

6. The teacher's lecture was good.

   _____ lecture was good.

GO ON TO THE NEXT PAGE

7. Here is Antoine's lunch.

Here is _____ lunch.

8. There is Mohammed's sweater.

There is _____ sweater.

9. This is Harry's brother.

This is _____ brother.

10. That is the cat's milk.

That is _____ milk.

STOP   CHECK ANSWERS ON PAGE 144.

THE PRONOUNS *WHO*, *WHOM*, AND *WHOSE*

Read the following:

Who told you that?
About whom are you speaking?
Whose pet is that?

Did you notice?

The pronoun **who**, **whom**, and **whose** can be used to ask questions.
The pronoun **who** is the subject of a sentence.
The pronoun **whom** is used after words like **about**, **against**, **around**, **before**, **below**, **beneath**, **between**, **for**, **of**, **on**, **to**, **under**, and **with**.
The pronoun **whose** is used to show ownership.

Try it out. Fill in each blank with **who**, **whom**, or **whose**.

1. For _____ do you work?

2. _____ sister are you?

3. _____ told you that?

4. About _____ are you talking?

5. _____ gave that to you?

6. With _____ are they going?

7. _____ wants me to stay?

8. _____ name is Jane?

9. _____ house is this?

10. _____ is not working today?

STOP   CHECK ANSWERS ON PAGE 144.

THE VERBS *LAY, LAYS, LAID, WILL LAY, HAS LAID, HAVE LAID,* AND *HAD LAID*

Read the following:	Andy lays it on the table. He laid it on the table. I will lay it on the table. She has laid it on the table. He had laid it on the table.	Andy and Ann lay it on the table. They laid it on the table. We will lay it on the table. They have laid it on the table. They had laid it on the table.
Did you notice?	The verbs **lays** and **lay** describe action in the present. **Lay** goes with plural nouns and the pronouns **I, you, we,** and **they**. **Lays** goes with singular nouns and the pronouns **he, she,** and **it**. The word **laid** describes action in the past. The words **will lay** describe action in the future. **Laid** goes with the helping verbs **has, have,** and **had**.	
Did you know?	**Lay** means **put** or **place**. It should not be confused with **lie**, which means **recline**.	

Try it out.	Fill in each blank with the correct form of the verb **lay**.

1. _____ the bundles on the table.

2. Hens _____ eggs.

3. I can't remember where you _____ your wallet yesterday.

4. He had _____ the wood there before I arrived.

5. Mary usually _____ her mail on the table these days.

6. Yesterday we _____ the mirror in a safe place.

7. My hen _____ many eggs last week.

8. He had _____ his eyeglasses on the sofa before he sat down.

9. I have _____ many things in wrong places.

10. The dog _____ its bone on the kitchen floor earlier.

STOP   CHECK ANSWERS ON PAGE 145.

CONTRACTIONS

| **Try it out.** | Write the contractions for the following words. |

1. he will _____   11. did not _____

2. it will _____   12. could not _____

3. should not _____   13. cannot _____

4. will not _____   14. I will _____

5. they will _____   15. we will _____

6. do not _____   16. have not _____

7. has not _____   17. is not _____

8. was not _____   18. were not _____

9. are not _____   19. would not _____

10. had not _____   20. she will _____

STOP CHECK ANSWERS ON PAGE 145.

WRITING THE TIME OF DAY

Read the following:	She will arrive at 5:35 P.M. tomorrow. We are taking the train at 6:25 A.M. tomorrow.
Do you remember?	**A.M.** and **P.M.** are written with capital letters and periods. There is a colon (:) between the hour and the minutes in the time. **A.M.** is after midnight and before noon. **P.M.** is after noon and before midnight.

Try it out.   Write the following times correctly.

1. 210 pm _____

2. 1205 pm _____

3. 325 am _____

4. 1015 am _____

5. 215 am _____

6. 105 am _____

7. 912 am _____

8. 345 pm _____

9. 714 am _____

10. 905 pm _____

STOP   CHECK ANSWERS ON PAGE 145.

WRITING PARAGRAPHS

Read the following: Manuel was at a point in life that forced him to make difficult decisions. **In the past**, he had avoided making tough choices. **Before**, he did what his parents told him was best or what his wife thought was best. **Now**, since the accident, he had no one to tell him what to do. **So** he would have to decide for himself about his children. **On the one hand**, he wanted to keep them, himself, even though it would be nearly impossible. **On the other hand**, it might be better for them to be raised by a foster family. **Unfortunately**, he had to make his decision soon.

Did you notice?   The underlined sentence in the paragraph is an **introductory sentence**.
It tells you the subject of the paragraph.
The other sentences tell more about Manuel and his decision making.
The sentences are **linked** to each other.
The words in dark print link the sentences together. They help to make it clear how one sentence relates to the other sentences.
Linked sentences make the paragraph flow and give it order.
The last sentence is a **conclusion** for the paragraph.

Did you know?   These words are often used to link sentences in a paragraph:

before	besides	finally	first
for example	fortunately	however	in addition
instead	in the past	meanwhile	next
now	on the other hand		nevertheless
so	then	therefore	unfortunately

| **Try it out.** | Read the following paragraph. Underline the words that link the sentences together.

Maxine needs help. Unfortunately, she does not admit it. Before, Maxine used to wonder aloud whether she was drinking too much. Now, even though she drinks more, she thinks she drinks moderately. Finally, either Maxine will stop denying her alcoholism, or drink will rule her life until she dies.

STOP   CHECK ANSWERS ON PAGE 145.

ORGANIZING SENTENCES INTO A PARAGRAPH

Read the following: Second, she can leave work early on school days so she will not get to class late. Now, with all these things in her favor, Kim is looking forward to earning more money at a better job one day soon. First, her older children are responsible, so she can leave them alone with the younger children. Kim finally has everything lined up so that she can go to night school to learn word processing. Finally, because she won a partial scholarship, she can now afford the tuition.

Did you notice?   The paragraph does not make sense.
The sentences are out of order.

Now read this: Kim finally has everything lined up so that she can go to night school to learn word processing. First, her older children are responsible, so she can leave them alone with the younger children. Second, she can leave work early on school days, so she will not get to class late. Finally, because she won a partial scholarship, she can now afford the tuition. Now, with all these things in her favor, Kim is looking forward to earning more money at a better job one day soon.

Did you notice?   The first line of this paragraph is indented.
The paragraph makes sense.
The introductory sentence says that Kim can now go to night school.
That sentence tells you what the paragraph is about.
The next three sentences tell how night school is possible for Kim.
The words **First**, **Second**, and **Finally** link the sentences.
The last sentence concludes the paragraph.

GO ON TO THE NEXT PAGE

Try it out.	Write the following sentences over in a paragraph that makes sense. First, write the introductory sentence. Then add the other sentences in an order that is logical.

Now they are eager to find out in what other ways they are similar. However, they were raised in separate families and never saw each other until last week. Betty and Jane are identical twins. In addition, they are both talented at dancing, drawing, and guitar playing. Nevertheless, there are amazing similarities between them. For example, both of them are hairdressers.

_____

_____

_____

_____

_____

STOP CHECK SAMPLE PARAGRAPH ON PAGE 145.

PROOFREADING

Read the following:	Everyone in my family enjoys camping. we go camping for at least too Weeks evry sumer.
Did you notice?	There are errors in spelling and capitalizing in the above sentences.
Now read this:	Everyone in my <u>family</u> enjoys camping. <u>We</u> go camping for at least <u>two</u> <u>weeks</u> <u>every</u> <u>summer</u>.
Did you notice?	In the above sentences, all the errors are corrected. The words that were changed are underlined.
Did you know?	It is a good idea to **proofread** everything you write. When you proofread, you look for mistakes to correct. Two things to look for are mistakes in spelling and capitalizing.

Try it out. Proofread the following paragraph. Write the whole paragraph over with the mistakes corrected.

  our writing asignments are never very intresting. for example, at the begining of the term, we wrot about what we wanted to get out of the class. later, we wrote about difrent Holidays. sometimes we write about the whether or members of our Famlys. I would like to writ about some thing more exciteing.

_____

_____

_____

_____

_____

_____

_____

_____

_____

STOP CHECK ANSWERS ON PAGE 145.

SPELLING

| **Try it out.** | Look at each word. Then cover it and write it in the blank. Check your spelling. Finally, write a sentence using the word. |

1. health   _____

_____

2. shoes   _____

_____

3. sometimes   _____

_____

4. ache   _____

_____

5. straight   _____

_____

STOP   CHECK SAMPLE ANSWERS ON PAGE 145.

CAPITALIZING (HISTORICAL PERIODS AND DOCUMENTS)

Write each sentence over correctly.

1. the industrial revolution began in england over two hundred years ago.

   _____

   _____

2. we are living in the computer age.

   _____

3. A new system of government was set up by the american constitution.

   _____

   _____

4. the american revolution was different from the french revolution and the russian revolution.

   _____

   _____

5. the bill of rights protects the rights of each of us.

   _____

   _____

COMBINING SENTENCES

Write one sentence that combines the two in each of the following pairs. Use a comma with **or**, **but**, or **and** in the sentence you write.

1. Juana would like to go with you.
   She has to go to the dentist.

   _____

   _____

2. It has been raining for ten days.
   There haven't been any floods.

   _____

   _____

GO ON TO THE NEXT PAGE

3. We helped them yesterday.
They helped us today.

_____

_____

4. I borrowed my friend's car for a quick run to the store.
It ran out of gas on the way.

_____

_____

5. Do your work on time.
It will just become too much for you.

_____

_____

SENTENCE PARTS (INDEPENDENT AND DEPENDENT WORD GROUPS)

Underline the dependent word group in each of the following sentences.

1. We often get up late when we are on vacation.

2. After we had so much trouble, we didn't want to go.

3. No one called the hotel where they are staying.

4. Several people saw them yesterday while they were here.

5. Although it is very late, I am still going.

END MARKS (PUNCTUATION MARKS)

Put the correct end mark at the end of each sentence.

1. Sheila asked when she wanted to go

2. George asked when she was going to the store

3. Nobody wanted to ask why no one called the police

4. When did she arrive here

5. Harry asked who the woman was

GO ON TO THE NEXT PAGE

PRONOUNS (SHOWING OWNERSHIP OR BELONGING TO)

In each blank in the sentences, write a pronoun that shows ownership.

1. This is Sharon's coat.

   This coat is _____. This is _____ coat.

2. This is my apartment.

   This apartment is _____.

3. That is Ed's pen.

   That is _____ pen. That is _____.

4. My friends' party was lots of fun.

   _____ party was lots of fun.

5. The plant's roots are damaged.

   _____ roots are damaged.

THE PRONOUNS *WHO*, *WHOM*, AND *WHOSE*

Fill in each blank with **who**, **whom**, or **whose**.

1. To _____ did you give that?

2. _____ idea is this?

3. _____ spoke to you about this?

4. _____ helped you with this?

5. For _____ are you doing this?

THE VERBS *LAY, LAYS, LAID, WILL LAY, HAS LAID, HAVE LAID,* AND *HAD LAID*

Fill in each blank with the correct form of the verb **lay**.

1. Paul _____ his books on the table yesterday.

2. My hen _____ many eggs every week.

3. I _____ your package in a safe place tomorrow.

4. They have _____ things in the wrong places again.

5. Please _____ this down for me.

GO ON TO THE NEXT PAGE

CONTRACTIONS

Write the contractions for the following words.

1. I will _____
2. they will _____
3. should not _____
4. has not _____
5. does not _____

6. you will _____
7. she will _____
8. would not _____
9. have not _____
10. do not _____

WRITING THE TIME OF DAY

Write the following times correctly.

1. 205 am _____
2. 1205 pm _____
3. 810 am _____

4. 1010 pm _____
5. 525 am _____

WRITING PARAGRAPHS

Underline the words that link the sentences.

The blood supply was running low, so an appeal went to the public to give blood. However, there was almost no increase in the rate of blood donations after the appeal. People were afraid that giving blood might put them at risk for AIDS. Of course, giving blood does not put people at risk. In fact, receiving blood is not as risky now as it was a few years ago.

ORGANIZING SENTENCES INTO A PARAGRAPH

Write the following sentences over in a paragraph that makes sense. First, write the introductory sentence. Then add the other sentences in an order that is logical.

Because she always recommends dependable sitters, her service has become very popular. The idea for the service began to come to her when she got more requests to babysit than she could handle. Mrs. Tanaka has developed a thriving babysitting service. Later, for a small fee, she lined up babysitters for parents who needed them. As a result, she is so busy filling requests for sitters that she has no time to babysit anymore. In the beginning, she recommended babysitters she knew.

GO ON TO THE NEXT PAGE

_____

_____

_____

_____

_____

_____

PROOFREADING

Proofread the following paragraph. Write the whole paragraph over with the mistakes corrected.

i answerd an ad in the <u>new york times</u> for a job rescently. someone called me from the acme plumbing co. i was very nervose while i was being interviewed and i could hardley talk. Needless to say i did'nt get the job I need to practise going on interviews.

_____

_____

_____

_____

SPELLING

Use each of the following words in a sentence.

1. health

_____

2. shoes

_____

3. sometimes

_____

4. ache

_____

5. straight

_____

STOP CHECK ANSWERS BEGINNING ON PAGE 145.

93

Count how many items you answered correctly in each **Section** of the Chapter Four Review. Write your score per section in the **My Scores** column. If all of your section scores are as high as the **Good Scores**, go on to Chapter Five. If any of your section scores are lower than the **Good Scores**, study the lessons on the assigned **Review Pages** again before you go on to Chapter Five.

Section	Good Scores	My Scores	Review Pages
Capitalizing (Historical Periods and Documents)	4 or 5		72–73
Combining Sentences	4 or 5		74–75
Sentence Parts (Independent and Dependent Word Groups)	4 or 5		76
End Marks (Punctuation Marks)	4 or 5		77
Pronouns (Showing Ownership or Belonging To)	4 or 5		78–79
The Pronouns **Who**, **Whom**, and **Whose**	4 or 5		80
The Verbs **Lay**, **Lays**, **Laid**, **Will Lay**, **Has Laid**, **Have Laid**, and **Had Laid**	4 or 5		81
Contractions	8, 9, or 10		82
Writing the Time of Day	4 or 5		83
Writing Paragraphs	3		84
Organizing Sentences into a Paragraph	6		85–86
Proofreading	17–21		87
Spelling	4 or 5		88

CHAPTER FIVE

CAPITALIZING

Read the following:	SEASONS	GAMES	SUBJECTS	TITLES
	summer	football	arithmetic	mother
	fall	baseball	history	sister
	winter	chess	science	uncle
	spring	tennis	French	Aunt Maria

Did you notice?

The names of seasons and games are not capitalized.
The names of most subjects are not capitalized.
Subjects that are the names of languages are capitalized.
People's titles are not capitalized unless they are used with a name.

Try it out.   Write each sentence over correctly.

1. i am going west in the spring to visit my aunt kiyo.

2. jim and i are taking spanish and french in the fall.

3. during the football season, i am going to visit my cousin.

4. mei plays checkers and chess in the fall.

5. my uncle joe and his daughter love to play tennis.

6. my aunt says that spring is my uncle julio's favorite season.

7. on sunday our club is having a picnic in the western part of town.

8. i need help in english, spanish, and geography.

GO ON TO THE NEXT PAGE

9. football and basketball are my cousin's favorite sports.

_____

10. last spring we traveled east, and i met a famous actor.

_____

STOP   CHECK ANSWERS ON PAGE 146.

WORD ORDER IN SENTENCES

Try it out. Use the following groups of words to write sentences. Add necessary commas.

1. Together my well get sister brother and along wife.

   _____

2. My frightened fight terrible the at us office.

   _____

3. Shocked when were two hit each we the started men to other.

   _____

4. Office storm looked it our like had hit by been a.

   _____

5. On police when fight going arrived the the was still.

   _____

STOP CHECK ANSWERS ON PAGE 146.

PRONOUNS AND WHAT THEY REFER TO

Read the following:	John enjoys <u>his</u> children. Jennifer and Andrew love <u>their</u> kitten. The cat drank <u>its</u> milk quickly.
Did you notice?	The pronoun **his** refers to the proper noun **John**. The proper noun **John** comes before the pronoun **his**. The pronoun **their** refers to the proper nouns **Jennifer** and **Andrew**. The proper nouns **Jennifer** and **Andrew** come before the pronoun **their**. The pronoun **its** refers to the noun **cat**. The noun **cat** comes before the pronoun **its**.
Do you remember?	The pronouns **his**, **their**, and **its** show ownership.

Try it out. Fill in each blank with the correct pronoun.

1. My boyfriend sent _____ mother a present.

2. Dominique's brother left _____ job to become an actor.

3. The elephants in the circus lifted _____ trunks.

4. That car needs to have _____ door fixed.

5. Norio gave _____ girlfriend a ring.

6. The train blew _____ whistle.

7. They need _____ rest.

8. The men and women want _____ pay raise now.

9. Flora put _____ sweater on the chair.

10. We have had _____ lunch already.

STOP CHECK ANSWERS ON PAGE 146.

THE VERBS *LIE, LIES, LAY, WILL LIE, HAS LAIN, HAVE LAIN,* AND *HAD LAIN*

Read the following:	Bill lies in bed.	Bill and Ann lie in bed.
	He lay in bed.	They lay in bed.
	I will lie in bed.	We will lie in bed.
	She has lain in bed.	They have lain in bed.
	He had lain in bed.	They had lain in bed.

Did you notice? The verbs **lies** and **lie** describe action in the present.
Lie goes with plural nouns and the pronouns **I**, **you**, **we**, and **they**.
Lies goes with singular nouns and the pronouns **he**, **she**, and **it**.
The word **lay** describes action in the past.
The words **will lie** describe action in the future.
Lain goes with the helping verbs **has**, **have**, and **had**.

Did you know? **Lie** means **recline**.
It should not be confused with **lay**, which means **put** or **place**.

| **Try it out.** | Fill in each blank with the correct form of the verb **lie**. |

1. I must _____ down because I am tired.

2. Last week I _____ in bed every day until seven o'clock in the morning.

3. He _____ in bed all day if you let him.

4. Grace had _____ in bed for a long time before she regained her health.

5. They have _____ there since you put them there.

6. Tomorrow I _____ in bed most of the day.

7. He has _____ in the sun for an hour.

8. Dan _____ down for a nap every day after dinner.

9. Who has _____ here?

10. My cat _____ in the same spot all the time.

STOP CHECK ANSWERS ON PAGE 146.

THE VERBS *TEACH* AND *LEARN*

Read the following:	Please <u>teach</u> that to me. I want to <u>learn</u> it. She <u>taught</u> Ben how to read. Ben <u>learned</u> how to read.		
Did you notice?	**Teach** means **cause someone to know something**. **Learn** means **gain understanding of something**.		
Now read the following:	These are the forms of **teach** and **learn**:		

PRESENT	PAST	WITH **HAS**, **HAVE**, AND **HAD**
teach, teaches	taught	taught
learn, learns	learned	learned

| **Try it out.** | Fill in each blank with the correct form of **teach** or **learn**.

1. She _____ me how to do that yesterday.

2. I _____ that very well last week.

3. Don't _____ her such things.

4. My child can _____ anything.

5. Help me _____ her how to drive.

6. I _____ that from him earlier.

7. We _____ a lot from him over the years.

8. I _____ him everything he knows.

9. Miss Salazar _____ several classes at the Adult Center now.

10. Her students _____ a lot from her every day.

STOP   CHECK ANSWERS ON PAGE 146.

THE WORDS *ITS* AND *IT'S*, *THEIR* AND *THEY'RE*, AND *WHOSE* AND *WHO'S*

Read the following:

Whose coat is that?
Who's there?

This is their house.
They're not home now.

It's good to be here.
This is its food.

Do you remember?

Many words sound alike but are spelled differently and have different meanings.
Its, their, and **whose** show ownership.
It's means **it is** or **it has.**
They're means **they are.**
Who's means **who is** or **who has.**

Try it out.   Fill in each blank with the correct word.

1. _____ not mine. (**Its** or **It's**)

2. _____ name is that? (**Who's** or **Whose**)

3. _____ taken my coat? (**Who's** or **Whose**)

4. Is this _____ kitten? (**they're** or **their**)

5. _____ not at home. (**They're** or **Their**)

6. _____ car is this? (**Who's** or **Whose**)

7. _____ going with us. (**Their** or **They're**)

8. _____ sister is she? (**Who's** or **Whose**)

9. _____ hard to work and go to school at the same time. (**Its** or **It's**)

10. I don't think _____ nice to do that. (**its** or **it's**)

STOP   CHECK ANSWERS ON PAGE 147.

THE COMMA

Read the following:	Let's repaint the <u>ugly green</u> chair. My <u>little old</u> cat is tired.
	I like my <u>nice</u>, <u>warm</u> coat. This is a <u>pleasant</u>, <u>friendly</u> restaurant.
Do you remember?	There is no comma between two adjectives when the second adjective describes age, color, or size. There is usually a comma between two adjectives at other times.

Try it out. Each of the following sentences has two adjectives. Add commas between adjectives where they are needed. If a sentence needs no comma, write **NC** in the blank following the sentence.

1. She is a tired old woman. _____

2. Her little black kitten ran away. _____

3. It has been a long hard year. _____

4. The handsome kind boy is here. _____

5. I won't throw out my torn green jacket. _____

6. My itchy rough sweater is gone. _____

7. The frightened hurt man thanked us for our help. _____

8. The tired old dog looked at us. _____

9. We looked through the frosty cold window. _____

10. The healthy black cat stared at us. _____

STOP CHECK ANSWERS ON PAGE 147.

ORGANIZING SENTENCES INTO A PARAGRAPH

Read the following:

    In addition, they assembled the foods they would not find on the way. Pioneer families made long, hard journeys to the West. Such careful preparation helped many families reach their destinations. Therefore, they prepared carefully so that they could survive. First, they gathered plenty of warm, sturdy clothing. Finally, they chose only their cherished possessions to take, so they didn't have too much to carry.

Did you notice?

The paragraph does not make sense.
The sentences are out of order.

Now read this:

    Pioneer families made long, hard journeys to the West. Therefore, they prepared carefully so that they could survive. First, they gathered plenty of warm, sturdy clothing. In addition, they assembled the foods they would not find on the way. Finally, they chose only their cherished possessions to take, so they didn't have too much to carry. Such careful preparation helped many families reach their destinations.

Did you notice?

The paragraph makes sense.
The first line of the paragraph is indented.
The introductory sentence says the paragraph is about pioneer families' journeys.
In a logical order, the other sentences tell about the preparation for those journeys.
The words **Therefore**, **First**, **In addition**, and **Finally** link the sentences.

GO ON TO THE NEXT PAGE

| Try it out. | Write the following sentences over in a paragraph that makes sense. First, write the introductory sentence. Then add the other sentences in a logical order. |

Fortunately, he was athletic and would pass easily. David had no choice but to wait. Therefore, he had to reschedule his test. Unfortunately, no appointments were available for at least six months. David applied for a job with the police and was scheduled to take the physical strength test on Wednesday. However, the day before, he broke his foot.

_____

_____

_____

_____

_____

STOP   CHECK SAMPLE PARAGRAPH ON PAGE 147.

SENTENCE VARIETY

Read the following: His wife has died. Classes at the trade school are out of the question. Her income had been large. It had supported the whole family. He had planned to quit his job. He had planned to prepare for a different kind of work. Now he needs every penny he earns. He needs it just to get by. He may never get out of the trap he's in.

Now read this: Now that his wife has died, classes at the trade school are out of the question. Her income had been large enough to support the whole family. He had planned to quit his job and to prepare for a different kind of work. Now, however, he needs every penny he earns just to get by. He may never get out of the trap he's in.

Did you notice?   The sentences in the first paragraph are short and choppy.
They are all similar to each other.
The second paragraph is more pleasing to read.
The sentences in the second paragraph are varied.
Some are longer than others; some are combined.
There are some linking words in the second paragraph.

Try it out.   Write the following paragraph over to make it more pleasing to read.

My oldest brother is always in trouble with the law. He is now in a detention center. Our parents could not control him. Marriage has not helped him mature. My sisters are afraid of him. My other brothers are afraid of him. I am afraid of him. We wish we could find the thing to do that would make him straighten out.

_____

_____

_____

_____

_____

_____

STOP   CHECK SAMPLE PARAGRAPH ON PAGE 147.

SENTENCE VARIETY

Did you know?

Using these hints will help you write paragraphs that are pleasing to read:

- Use a variety of types of sentences: statements, questions, and commands.
- Vary the way sentences begin; don't always start with the subject.
- Write sentences of different lengths: some short, some longer.
- Use a variety of linking words, but don't overuse them.
- Write the most important points at the beginning of a paragraph.

Try it out.

Write the paragraph over to make it more pleasing to read. Use the above hints to help you.

The man was on the run. He wore a hat that covered his eyes. He wore a dark coat with the collar turned up. He wore glasses. They were dark glasses. He carried an old bag. The bag was torn. He walked swiftly. He kept looking over his shoulder. He kept one hand in his pocket. He heard a noise. He hid in the shadows of the night.

_____

_____

_____

_____

_____

_____

_____

_____

_____

_____

STOP CHECK SAMPLE PARAGRAPH ON PAGE 147.

PROOFREADING

Read the following: Kin doesnt want to work on the night shift but he have no choice Why should they have anything to say, He is'nt the employer. Besides hes new hear.

Did you notice? There are several kinds of errors in the sentences above.

Now read this: Kin doesn't want to work on the night shift, but he has no choice. Why should he have anything to say? He isn't the employer. Besides, he's new here.

Did you notice? In the above sentences, all the errors are corrected. The words and punctuation marks that were changed are underlined.

Did you know? When you proofread, you look for mistakes with periods, question marks, and commas.
You check the spelling of contractions.
You see whether the verbs and the pronouns are right.
You check all spelling and capitalizing.

Try it out. Proofread the following paragraph. It has many errors. Write the whole paragraph over with the mistakes corrected.

most Pilgrim child's lives in school wer'nt very easy. they usualy had strict Teachers when chilren talked in school he or she were punished. often they was whipped. the children were afraid of the teachers. They did'nt like school and they were glad when the Day was over.

_____

_____

_____

_____

_____

_____

_____

_____

STOP CHECK ANSWERS ON PAGE 147.

SPELLING

Read the following:
Try to <u>develop</u> a better plan.
Artie always uses good <u>judgment</u>.
We will do this <u>instead</u>.
I will <u>just</u> show <u>him</u> this.
I always <u>lose</u> my gloves.

Did you know?
The underlined words in the above sentences are often misspelled.

Try it out. Look at each word. Then cover it and write it in the blank. Check your spelling. Finally, write a sentence using the word.

1. develop _____

_____

2. judgment _____

_____

3. instead _____

_____

4. just _____

_____

5. lose _____

_____

STOP CHECK SAMPLE ANSWERS ON PAGE 147.

ALPHABETIZING (USING THE PHONE BOOK)

Do you remember?   A phone book has guide names at the top of each page.
The guide names are people's last names.
They tell which are the first and last names on that page.
All the names between the two guide names are on that page in alphabetical order.

Now read this: Here is a sample of the guide names at the top of a phone book page.

> **Smith—Sobel**

Did you notice?   The last name **Smith** is the first name on the page.
The last name **Sobel** is the last name on the page.

Try it out.   Use the guide names **Smith** and **Sobel** to answer the following questions. Write **yes** or **no** in each blank.

1. Is the name **Ben Snyder** on this page? _____

2. Is the name **Carl Smythe** on this page? _____

3. Is the name **Susan Snell** on this page? _____

4. Is the name **Laura Sobin** on this page? _____

5. Is the name **Sharon Snow** on this page? _____

6. Is the name **Frank Snead** on this page? _____

7. Is the name **José Sanchez** on this page? _____

8. Is the name **Pedro Santos** on this page? _____

9. Is the name **Andrea Sovo** on this page? _____

10. Is the name **Kim Sneel** on this page? _____

STOP   CHECK ANSWERS ON PAGE 147.

CAPITALIZING

Write each sentence over correctly.

1. in the fall, florence and i are going to the north to visit our cousins.

_____

_____

2. my italian cousin and my irish cousin are going to ireland and italy next spring.

_____

_____

3. lan and jim live on kean road and work with computers.

_____

_____

4. my mother and aunt joan went east to visit the statue of liberty.

_____

_____

5. my favorite season is the summer, and my favorite day is saturday.

_____

_____

WORD ORDER IN SENTENCES

Use the following groups of words to write sentences. Add necessary commas.

1. Boulevard hospital I and Gil Luz Tanako in work a Northern on.

_____

2. Deaths past a year odd the there been have great number of in.

_____

3. Poison many deadly elderly were a with injected patients.

_____

4. Nurse had died one of all care patients the before they taken.

_____

5. Nurses knew doctors the police and murderer who was the.

_____

PRONOUNS AND WHAT THEY REFER TO
Fill in each blank with the correct pronoun.

1. Ernesto left to go back to _____ other job.

2. They sent _____ own mother a present.

3. I want _____ dinner now.

4. The woman took _____ own child home.

5. The tree lost _____ leaves.

THE VERBS *LIE, LIES, LAY, WILL LIE, HAS LAIN, HAVE LAIN,* AND *HAD LAIN*
Fill in each blank with the correct form of the verb **lie**.

1. Larry has _____ in bed for hours.

2. I _____ in bed a long time yesterday.

3. Silvia _____ in bed every day for a nap.

4. Chai _____ in bed longer tomorrow.

5. _____ down and take a nap.

THE VERBS *TEACH* AND *LEARN*
Fill in each blank with the correct form of **teach** or **learn**.

1. Mrs. Russo _____ history in my daughter's school last year.

2. Mr. Brown _____ English for ten years now.

3. I _____ many things from my teachers years ago.

4. We _____ on our jobs now.

5. Tomiko _____ students at another school next year.

GO ON TO THE NEXT PAGE

THE WORDS *ITS* AND *IT'S*, *THEIR* AND *THEY'RE*, AND *WHOSE* AND *WHO'S*

Fill in each blank with the correct word.

1. _____ book is this? (**Who's** or **Whose**)

2. _____ in the room now? (**Who's** or **Whose**)

3. _____ going away soon. (**Their** or **They're**)

4. _____ not funny. (**It's** or **Its**)

5. I took off _____ coat. (**it's** or **its**)

THE COMMA

Each of the following sentences has two adjectives. Add commas between adjectives where they are needed. If a sentence needs no comma, write **NC** in the blank following the sentence.

1. Please hold my cute little kitten for me. _____

2. The ugly bare room needs decorating. _____

3. The slender curly-haired woman laughed loudly. _____

4. My dear old mother is not feeling well. _____

5. The lost scared girl stared blindly at us. _____

ORGANIZING SENTENCES INTO A PARAGRAPH

Write the following sentences over in a paragraph that makes sense. First, write the introductory sentence. Then add the other sentences in a logical order.

While he was eating breakfast, he thought about all the bills that had to be paid and the other constant expenses. He lay in bed until his wife said that things would work out, no matter what happened. Finally, he was ready to go, but he wasn't prepared to find out whether he was one of the two hundred to be laid off today. That helped him gather the courage to get ready for work. Mike had a nerve-wracking day ahead of him, and he didn't want to get up.

_____

_____

_____

_____

_____

GO ON TO THE NEXT PAGE

SENTENCE VARIETY

Write the following paragraphs over to make them more pleasing to read.

I am thirty-five years old. I still live at home with my mother and my father and my sister. I still have the same room I had when I was a child. I still do the same things. My chances of meeting someone are not very good. My chances of getting married are not good. The older I get, the more unhappy I get.

I need to get my own apartment. My parents get upset when I talk about doing this. They think I am still a child. They treat me as if I were a child. Obviously, there must be something wrong with me. I have an excellent job. I earn good money. I want to be independent. I am afraid to leave home.

_____

_____

_____

_____

_____

_____

_____

_____

_____

_____

_____

_____

_____

_____

GO ON TO THE NEXT PAGE

PROOFREADING

Proofread the following paragraph. It has many errors. Write the whole paragraph over with the mistakes corrected.

have you evr sen an empyt house and wondred who had lived ther. whenevr i woud have to walk past a certin house in my neigborhod i woud cros the street and walk on the othr side. the hous has ben borded up for as long as i can rember. everyone talk about the house in hushed voics. some say drakula lived ther. frankly i dont take any chancs. i just dont walk pas the house.

_____

_____

_____

_____

_____

_____

_____

_____

_____

SPELLING

Use each of the following words in a sentence.

1. develop

_____

2. judgment

_____

3. instead

_____

4. just

_____

5. lose

_____

GO ON TO THE NEXT PAGE

ALPHABETIZING (USING THE PHONE BOOK)

Use the guide names **Rodrigez** and **Rubino** to answer these questions. Write **Yes** or **No** in each blank.

1. Is the name **Robert Rueben** on this page? _____

2. Is the name **Rodrico Rodez** on this page? _____

3. Is the name **Mary Rogers** on this page? _____

4. Is the name **Sally Robins** on this page? _____

5. Is the name **Harry Rubin** on this page? _____

STOP CHECK ANSWERS ON BEGINNING PAGE 147.

Count how many items you answered correctly in each **Section** of the Chapter Five Review. Write your score per section in the **My Scores** column. If all of your section scores are as high as the **Good Scores**, take the Posttest. If any of your section scores are lower than the **Good Scores**, study the lessons on the assigned **Review Pages** again before you take the Posttest.

Section	Good Scores	My Scores	Review Pages
Capitalizing	4 or 5		96–97
Word Order in Sentences	4 or 5		98
Pronouns and What They Refer To	4 or 5		99
The Verbs **Lie, Lies, Lay, Will Lie, Has Lain, Have Lain,** and **Had Lain**	4 or 5		100
The Verbs **Teach** and **Learn**	4 or 5		101
The Words **Its** and **It's, Their** and **They're**, and **Whose** and **Who's**	4 or 5		102
The Comma	4 or 5		103
Organizing Sentences into a Paragraph	5		104–105
Sentence Variety	Correct paragraphs		106–107
Proofreading	30–37		108
Spelling	4 or 5		109
Alphabetizing (Using the Phone Book)	4 or 5		110

CAPITALIZING

Here is a list of nouns. Correct any nouns that are not written correctly. Put a **C** in the blank by those that are correct.

1. spanish _____
2. Winter _____
3. south Carolina _____
4. rev. James Corbett _____
5. South _____
6. Island _____
7. governor _____
8. Grammar _____
9. Place _____
10. Mother _____

SINGULAR AND PLURAL SUBJECTS

Underline the nouns and pronouns that control the verb in each of the following sentences. Write **S** in the blank if the subject of the sentence is singular. Write **P** in the blank if the subject is plural.

1. My husband's relatives are all greedy. _____
2. Everybody is here today. _____
3. Nobody was there before. _____
4. The ministers' meeting was yesterday. _____
5. Anyone can do that. _____

RECOGNIZING SENTENCES

Put a check (√) by each of the sentences.

☐ 1. Talk more softly.
☐ 2. While I was at the bus station.
☐ 3. After we ate a big dinner.
☐ 4. Until I arrived.
☐ 5. Are you certain about this?

GO ON TO THE NEXT PAGE

WORD ORDER IN SENTENCES

Use the following groups of words to write sentences. Add necessary commas.

1. On trip Ken Manual I hunting together and Koyi went a.

   _____

2. Brought sandwiches salads with snacks we lots drinks and of us.

   _____

3. Grounds when to hunting we gear our we the unpacked got.

   _____

4. Set tents we up and rest sat our down to then first we.

   _____

5. Us suddenly deer run we past right three saw.

   _____

COMBINING SENTENCES

Write one sentence that combines the two in each of the following pairs. Use a comma with **or**, **but**, or **and** in the sentence you write.

1. My friend José left his country.
   He came to the United States of America.

   _____

   _____

2. He had to come to this country.
   His enemies would have killed him.

   _____

   _____

3. José is an illegal alien.
   He does not have a job.

   _____

   _____

4. He is learning English.
   No one will hire him.

   _____

   _____

GO ON TO THE NEXT PAGE

5. José is not happy here.
It is too dangerous for him to return to his country.

_____

_____

SHORTENING SENTENCES

Shorten the following sentences by using commas.

1. Her friend Pedro and her friend Leonardo and her friend David and her friend Raul have their own band.

_____

_____

2. The mayor asked the police and the fire fighters and the transit workers and the sanitation workers to a party.

_____

_____

3. Elena is studying for an English test and Fabio is studying for an English test and Harue is studying for an English test and I am studying for an English test.

_____

_____

4. I listen to the radio a lot and I read papers a lot and I watch television a lot.

_____

_____

5. Peter likes funny movies and funny stories and funny jokes.

_____

_____

SENTENCE PARTS

Here are some sentence parts and some sentences. Underline each of the sentence parts. Put a check (√) by each of the sentences.

☐ **1.** When he does such thing.

☐ **2.** Who knows her?

☐ **3.** Who the man is.

☐ **4.** Until I can see him.

☐ **5.** How well do you know him?

GO ON TO THE NEXT PAGE

SENTENCE PARTS (INDEPENDENT AND DEPENDENT WORD GROUPS)

Underline the dependent word group in each of the following sentences.

1. Aliens can become citizens if they have been here a certain number of years.

2. Unless they learn English, they will have problems here.

3. Many aliens are becoming citizens after they learn English.

4. It is difficult for some aliens because people take advantage of them.

5. Many aliens have high hopes when they come here.

DIRECT QUOTATIONS

Write these direct quotations correctly. Add the correct end mark.

1. Gary said that does not belong here

_____

2. Christine asked why aren't you doing your work

_____

3. Robert said the computer is not working properly

_____

4. Arthur asked are you interested in some good advice

_____

5. Terry asked will this make a lot of money

_____

DIRECT AND INDIRECT QUOTATIONS

The following sentences contain indirect quotations. Write each sentence over so that it contains a direct quotation.

1. Adela said that she loves her new house.

_____

2. Mr. Petridis said that he wants his people to work harder.

_____

3. Miss Vega said that she needs to study this some more.

_____

GO ON TO THE NEXT PAGE

4. I said that I do not have any time for that.

_____

5. Hiroshi said that he is very lucky to have such a good job.

_____

END MARKS (PUNCTUATION MARKS)
Put the proper end mark at the end of each sentence.

1. He asked whether we had a chance

2. They said that we didn't

3. Why don't we have a chance

4. The manager asked why we were interested in trying out

5. We asked why he had to know

PRONOUNS
Fill in each blank with the correct pronoun.

1. _____ likes _____. (**me** and **he**)

2. _____ helped _____. (**us** and **they**)

3. _____ hurt _____. (**her** and **he**)

4. _____ knows _____. (**she** and **him**)

5. _____ saw _____. (**them** and **we**)

PRONOUNS AND WHAT THEY REFER TO
Fill in each blank with the correct pronoun.

1. Antoine lost _____ hat.

2. The workers began _____ lunch hour.

3. Giovanna changed _____ dress.

4. Alfredo found _____ wallet in the trunk of the car.

5. I love _____ own family.

GO ON TO THE NEXT PAGE

PRONOUNS (SHOWING OWNERSHIP OR BELONGING TO)

Fill in each blank with a pronoun that shows ownership.

1. Here is my cup.

   This cup is _____ .

2. That was Mike's sweater.

   That sweater was _____ .

3. The stone hit Sarah's leg.

   The stone hit _____ leg.

4. My parents' apartment is very small.

   _____ apartment is very small.

5. Here is the dog's leash.

   Here is _____ leash.

THE PRONOUNS *ANYBODY, ANYONE, EVERYBODY, EVERYONE, NOBODY, NO ONE, SOMEBODY,* AND *SOMEONE*

Underline the verb that is correct for the sentence.

1. Nobody (**seem** or **seems**) happy at this job.

2. Everybody (**belong** or **belongs**) here.

3. Somebody (**is** or **are**) being very nasty.

4. Everyone (**know** or **knows**) this is a joke.

5. Anybody (**have** or **has**) the power to do that.

THE WORDS *WHO, WHOM,* AND *WHOSE*

Fill in each blank with **who**, **whom**, or **whose**.

1. _____ pocketbook is this?

2. _____ is going to watch the children?

3. _____ hit you?

4. For _____ is this?

5. With _____ are you going?

GO ON TO THE NEXT PAGE

MORE THAN ONE (PLURAL)

Write the plural form of each of the following nouns.

1. dish _____
2. rock _____
3. tooth _____
4. tax _____
5. spy _____

6. shelf _____
7. deer _____
8. stitch _____
9. lunch _____
10. calf _____

ADJECTIVES AND LINKING VERBS

Fill in each blank in the sentences with an adjective from the list. Use each adjective **only once**.

ADJECTIVE LIST

delicious   loud   prettier   sour   well

1. The lemon tastes _____.
2. The band sounds _____.
3. The food smells _____.
4. I feel _____.
5. Laura looks _____ today than yesterday.

REGULAR AND IRREGULAR VERBS

Write two forms for each verb: the form for past and the form for up to now (with **has**).

REGULAR VERBS				IRREGULAR VERBS		
	PAST	UP TO NOW			PAST	UP TO NOW
1. look	_____	_____	6. teach		_____	_____
2. learn	_____	_____	7. write		_____	_____
3. try	_____	_____	8. go		_____	_____
4. plant	_____	_____	9. lay		_____	_____
5. lie	_____	_____	10. steal		_____	_____

GO ON TO THE NEXT PAGE

THE VERB *BE*

Fill in each blank with the correct form of the verb **be**.

1. Mary _____ going out with her boyfriend for years.

2. He _____ not very dependable now.

3. Everybody _____ at our house yesterday except for him.

4. Nobody _____ here for days.

5. We _____ there before.

THE VERBS *SPEAK, SPEAKS, SPOKE, WILL SPEAK, HAS SPOKEN, HAVE SPOKEN*, AND *HAD SPOKEN*

Fill in each blank with the correct form of the verb **speak**.

1. Harry _____ to me earlier.

2. My boss _____ to us later.

3. My baby _____ very well now.

4. Yoshiaki and I have _____ about it.

5. Manolo _____ to me yesterday.

THE VERBS *STEAL, STEALS, STOLE, WILL STEAL, HAS STOLEN, HAVE STOLEN*, AND *HAD STOLEN*

Fill in each blank with the correct form of the verb **steal**.

1. Mike _____ a pack of cigarettes from the store before.

2. Mike _____ a lot now.

3. He has _____ a number of things.

4. I'm sure Mike _____ something later.

5. Before he was ten years old, he had _____ a watch.

THE VERBS *WRITE, WRITES, WROTE, WILL WRITE, HAS WRITTEN, HAVE WRITTEN*, AND *HAD WRITTEN*

Fill in each blank with the correct form of the verb **write**.

1. We _____ to each other every day.

2. Tina _____ to me a month ago.

3. I _____ to you very soon.

4. Mr. Stanton insisted he had _____ the letter.

5. Lisa has _____ to me for years.

GO ON TO THE NEXT PAGE

THE VERBS *LAY, LAYS, LAID, WILL LAY, HAS LAID, HAVE LAID,* AND *HAD LAID*

Fill in each blank with the correct form of the verb **lay**.

1. I _____ the bags of groceries on the table before.

2. They have _____ their pencils on their desks.

3. My hen _____ very few eggs, as a rule.

4. Don _____ all his vacation clothes on his bed soon.

5. _____ everything on the table.

THE VERBS *LIE, LIES, LAY, WILL LIE, HAS LAIN, HAVE LAIN,* AND *HAD LAIN*

Fill in each blank with the correct form of the verb **lie**.

1. I _____ on my couch all day tomorrow.

2. Derrick has _____ there for hours.

3. My cat _____ in the same spot all the time.

4. _____ down for a while.

5. He _____ in bed all day yesterday.

THE VERBS *TEACH* AND *LEARN*

Fill in each blank with the correct form of **teach** or **learn**.

1. Maria _____ new jobs quickly and can soon do them on her own.

2. At school Ms. Kato _____ people to speak English now.

3. The teacher has also _____ many things from her pupils.

4. Ms. Castillo _____ at another school last year.

5. I _____ something new from her yesterday.

ADVERBS

In each blank, write the comparing form of the adverb correctly.

1. Karl spoke _____ of her than of him. (**highly**)

2. I see things _____ now than before. (**clearly**)

3. The dog growled the _____ of any dog I have every heard. (**fiercely**)

4. Tara danced the _____ of anyone. (**well**)

5. Andrew skates the _____ of all on the team. (**fast**)

GO ON TO THE NEXT PAGE

SHOWING OWNERSHIP OR BELONGING TO (POSSESSION)

The nouns that show ownership in these sentences are written incorrectly. Find each of those nouns and write their correct forms in the blanks.

1. We are meeting our childs' teacher soon. _____

2. The arrow hit the deers' leg. _____

3. James father is visiting him now. _____

4. The spys gun was taken by someone. _____

5. The watchs' minute hand is broken. _____

THE WORDS *ITS* AND *IT'S*, *THEIR* AND *THEY'RE*, AND *WHOSE* AND *WHO'S*

Fill in each blank with the correct word.

1. _____ fur looks peculiar. (**It's** or **Its**)

2. _____ cat is this? (**Whose** or **Who's**)

3. _____ had time to do this? (**Whose** or **Who's**)

4. _____ name is on the bill. (**They're** or **Their**)

5. _____ not going to go with us. (**They're** or **Their**)

THE COMMA

Add commas in the following sentences where they are needed. If a sentence needs no comma, write **NC** in the blank following the sentence.

1. Of course I'm buying that new white car. _____

2. Indeed it is a nice friendly little kitten. _____

3. This has been a long hard year. _____

4. This is my new blue hat. _____

5. Certainly this is good sturdy furniture. _____

ABBREVIATIONS (SHORTENED WORDS)

Fill in each blank with the correct abbreviation.

1. _____ William Smith's church is on Webster _____ near

   the Forbes _____ . (**Reverend**; **Avenue**; **Company**)

GO ON TO THE NEXT PAGE

2. I will go to _____ Berger's office on River _____ at 10:45 _____. (**Doctor; Road; in the morning**)

3. _____ Peter Mendez visited the Bakers on Dover _____. (**Reverend; Drive**)

4. At 8:00 _____ today, _____ Jones starts work at the hospital on Baker _____. (**in the morning; Doctor; Street**)

5. The Ford _____ may not be on Eastern _____. (**Company; Boulevard**)

CONTRACTIONS

Write the contractions for the following words.

1. I have _____

2. she is _____

3. does not _____

4. will not _____

5. it is _____

6. you will _____

7. would not _____

8. cannot _____

9. we are _____

10. it will _____

WRITING THE TIME OF DAY

Write the following times correctly.

1. 525 pm _____

2. 105 am _____

3. 330 pm _____

4. 1110 am _____

5. 730 pm _____

6. 1045 pm _____

7. 615 pm _____

8. 725 am _____

9. 415 pm _____

10. 850 am _____

THE WORDS A AND AN

Put **a** or **an** before each of the following.

1. _____ apron

2. _____ unbuilt house

3. _____ ice bag

4. _____ hug

5. _____ agreement

6. _____ union card

7. _____ helper

8. _____ unkind man

9. _____ illegal alien

10. _____ hill

GO ON TO THE NEXT PAGE

WRITING PARAGRAPHS

Underline the words that link the sentences in the following paragraph.

Rosa has been unhappily married for thirty years. In spite of her unhappiness, Rosa has never considered divorce. It would be unthinkable, especially since she is a mother and a grandmother. Moreover, if she had considered it, she would have been the first woman in her family to have done so. Therefore, since Rosa feels about divorce as she does, she may go to the grave an unhappy wife.

ORGANIZING SENTENCES INTO A PARAGRAPH

Write the following sentences over in a paragraph that makes sense. First, write the introductory sentence. Then add the other sentences in a logical order.

Immediately, she realized that she did not want to live with any of her children. Not long after her last daughter moved out, Rosa felt as though she could not stand living in the same house alone with her husband for another minute. After a few minutes of such thoughts, Rosa put on her apron, sighed, and set the table for two. At the same time, she began to wonder what it would be like if she just left. In addition, she became aware that she might have trouble supporting herself.

_____

_____

_____

_____

_____

_____

_____

_____

_____

GO ON TO THE NEXT PAGE

SENTENCE VARIETY

Write the following paragraph over to make it more pleasing to read.

A nervous man entered the diner. He looked around angrily. He was wearing a suit. It was a bit large for him. He looked evil. There were people in the diner. They were having their supper. They began to feel uncomfortable. Before the man walked in, they had been talking about the jail break. All day newscasters talked about it. They kept saying that the escaped convict was armed. They said he was dangerous. The tension rose in the diner. It made everyone nervous. Something was going to happen.

_____

_____

_____

_____

_____

_____

_____

PROOFREADING

Rewrite the following paragraph correctly.

i met a incredble persan the othr day. he cam here from el salvdor a numbr of Year ago. he work hard nd earned enugh mony to brin his family here. today he have his own Bussines, his own Car, and his own Home. now he help other peopl who come here from his Country. everybody Love him.

_____

_____

_____

_____

_____

_____

_____

GO ON TO THE NEXT PAGE

WRITING AN INVITATION

Write a letter to invite someone to a graduation party.

WRITING A BUSINESS LETTER

You ordered some boots. Write a letter to complain that you received the wrong boots. The boots were advertised in the <u>Chicago Globe</u>. You do not know the name of the president of the department store. Write to the **president, Hoover's Department Store, 211 Main Boulevard, Chicago, Illinois 60606**.

SPELLING

Spell the following words correctly.

1. piknik _____
2. neme _____
3. goodbuy _____
4. hellth _____
5. insted _____
6. becuz _____
7. ake _____
8. straght _____
9. couff _____
10. shos _____

11. cosin _____
12. onle _____
13. agin _____
14. jist _____
15. jugement _____
16. somtimes _____
17. sinse _____
18. coler _____
19. recive _____
20. develope _____

ALPHABETIZING (USING THE PHONE BOOK)

Use the guide names **Schramm** and **Schrun** to answer the questions. Write **Yes** or **No** in the blanks.

1. Is the name **Betty Schrer** on this page? _____
2. Is the name **Paul Schrall** on this page? _____
3. Is the name **Alan Schriber** on this page? _____
4. Is the name **William Schrom** on this page? _____
5. Is the name **Ann Schrum** on this page? _____

STOP CHECK ANSWERS BEGINNING ON PAGE 148.

Count how many items you answered correctly in each **Section** of the Posttest. Write your score per section in the **My Scores** column. If all of your section scores are as high as the **Good Scores**, go on to *Power English 8,* Chapter One. If any of your section scores are lower than the **Good Scores**, study the lessons on the assigned **Review Pages** again before you go on to *Power English 8,* Chapter One.

Section	Good Scores	My Scores	Review Pages
Capitalizing	8, 9, or 10		2–3, 26, 48, 72–73, 96–97
Singular and Plural Subjects	4 or 5		4
Recognizing Sentences	4 or 5		5
Word Order in Sentences	4 or 5		98
Combining Sentences	4 or 5		7, 27, 49–52, 74–75
Shortening Sentences	4 or 5		28
Sentence Parts	4 or 5		6, 29
Sentence Parts (Independent and Dependent Word Groups)	4 or 5		30, 53, 76
Direct Quotations	4 or 5		8, 31
Direct and Indirect Quotations	4 or 5		32–33
End Marks (Punctuation Marks)	4 or 5		9, 77
Pronouns	4 or 5		34
Pronouns and What They Refer To	4 or 5		99
Pronouns (Showing Ownership or Belonging To)	4 or 5		78–79
The Pronouns **Anybody, Anyone, Everybody, Everyone, Nobody, No One, Somebody,** and **Someone**	4 or 5		55
The Words **Who, Whom,** and **Whose**	4 or 5		80

Section	Good Scores	My Scores	Review Pages
More Than One (Plural)	8, 9, or 10		35
Adjectives and Linking Verbs	4 or 5		10
Regular and Irregular Verbs	8, 9, or 10		11
The Verb **Be**	4 or 5		12
The Verbs **Speak, Speaks, Spoke, Will Speak, Has Spoken, Have Spoken**, and **Had Spoken**	4 or 5		13
The Verbs **Steal, Steals, Stole, Will Steal, Has Stolen, Have Stolen**, and **Had Stolen**	4 or 5		36
The Verbs **Write, Writes, Wrote, Will Write, Has Written, Have Written**, and **Had Written**	4 or 5		56
The Verbs **Lay, Lays, Laid, Will Lay, Has Laid, Have Laid**, and **Had Laid**	4 or 5		81
The Verbs **Lie, Lies, Lay, Will Lie, Has Lain, Have Lain**, and **Had Lain**	4 or 5		100
The Verbs **Teach** and **Learn**	4 or 5		101
Adverbs	4 or 5		37
Showing Ownership or Belonging To (Possession)	4 or 5		38, 57
The Words **Its** and **It's**, **Their** and **They're**, and **Whose** and **Who's**	4 or 5		102
The Comma	4 or 5		58, 103
Abbreviations (Shortened Words)	4 or 5		59
Contractions	8, 9, or 10		39
Writing the Time of Day	8, 9, or 10		83
The Words **A** and **An**	8, 9, or 10		14
Writing Paragraphs	3		84
Organizing Sentences into a Paragraph	5		85–86, 104–105

Section	Good Scores	My Scores	Review Pages
Sentence Variety	A good paragraph		106–107
Proofreading	22–28		87, 108
Writing an Invitation	A correct letter		15–16
Writing a Business Letter	A correct letter		60–61
Spelling	16–20		17, 40, 62, 88, 109
Alphabetizing (Using the Phone Book)	4 or 5		63, 110

ANSWERS

Chapter 1

Capitalizing (Names of Magazines) (pp. 2–3)

1. Sally and I love to read <u>Ladies Home Companion</u> on Saturdays.
2. Pedro just finished reading Mark Twain's <u>Tom Sawyer</u>.
3. The last Wednesday in February, Bonnie, Cheryl, and I are going to Chicago.
4. Jim and I love the pictures in <u>National Geographic</u>.
5. <u>Fortune</u> is a magazine about our nation's business.
6. <u>US News and World Report</u> is an interesting magazine.
7. On February 11 I am traveling to China to learn Chinese.
8. President Ortez of Benson College asked Senator Brown to give the opening address in Spanish.
9. On Mother's Day we are sending our mother to France.
10. My favorite magazine is <u>Popular Mechanics</u>.

Singular and Plural Subjects (p. 4)

You should have a line under the following.

1. Bob, I (P)
2. We (P)
3. It (S)
4. Miss Hansen (S)
5. Someone (S)
6. Everyone (S)
7. mice (P)
8. day (S)
9. Everybody (S)
10. present (S)

Recognizing Sentences (p. 5)

You should have a check by each of the following.
1. Please hold the door for us.
2. The men are going to be here soon.
3. Run fast.
4. Drop that here.
6. Hold onto that.
10. Who told you that?

Sentence Parts (p. 6)

You should have a line under the following.
1. Even though I am not going.
4. Before Carl does anything.
7. When we were there.
8. Where they are going.
9. Until you say that.
10. Since that took place.
You should have a check by the following.
2. Did you send him here?
3. Who is there?
5. How much is that?
6. Stop doing that.

Combining Sentences (p. 7)

1. I am thinking of quitting my job, and my husband wants a change also.
2. We are not getting ahead here, and it is hard making ends meet.
3. Our children like it here, and my parents live close to us.
4. My parents want us to stay, and our friends are upset about our leaving.
5. We probably won't do anything, and my husband and I will remain here.

Direct Quotations (p. 8)

1. Sachiko said, "Please help me fix this."
2. Donna said, "I need more help."
3. José said, "Steve and I are going to the party."
4. Miss Eng said, "Please give the child her coat."
5. Maria said, "This is very heavy."
6. Bob said, "Last year was a hard one for me."
7. Paolo said, "No, I will not go."
8. Mr. Darbari said, "Call Joe and tell him to meet us."
9. Jennifer said, "My friends are visiting me soon."
10. Leila said, "It is fun being a judge."

End Marks (Punctuation Marks) (p. 9)

1. Which person said that?
2. How terrible that is!
3. Clara and Daniella are going to a show.
4. Please turn that around.
5. Hold that person.
   or: Hold that person!
6. How do you feel today?
7. Try to behave yourself.
8. What a wonderful day this is!
9. I never asked him anything.
10. Will you be here tomorrow?

Adjectives and Linking Verbs (p. 10)

1. brighter
2. well
3. happier
4. fresher
5. shiniest
6. best
7. taller
8. terrible
9. happiest
10. softer

Regular and Irregular Verbs (p. 11)

1. worked; has worked
2. chased; has chased
3. played; has played
4. cried; has cried
5. dressed; has dressed
6. ran; has run
7. caught; has caught
8. knew; has known
9. drank; has drunk
10. took; has taken

The Verb *Be* (p. 12)

1. was	5. has been	8. is
2. am	6. will be	9. have been
3. were	7. has been	10. was
4. are		

The Verbs *Speak, Speaks, Spoke, Will Speak, Has Spoken, Have Spoken,* and *Had Spoken* (p. 13)

1. have spoken	5. spoken	8. will speak
2. spoken	6. spoke	9. spoken
3. will speak	7. spoken	10. spoke
4. speaks		

The Words *A* and *An* (p. 14)

1. an idea	11. an oil well
2. a big ape	12. a half-hour
3. an older child	13. an even line
4. a tired man	14. a young man
5. an oak	15. a house
6. a pet	16. an uncle
7. an island	17. an actor
8. an onion	18. a yard
9. a bicycle	19. an Easter egg
10. a handsome man	20. an x-ray

Writing an Invitation (pp. 15–16)

Sample Letter:

November 11, 1990

Dear Mike,

   I just moved into a new apartment and am inviting a few friends for dinner. The housewarming party is Saturday, November 28, at 7:30 P.M. I hope you can make it.

   My new address is 21 Flower Lane, and my new phone number is 555-1256.

   Please phone by November 23 to tell me if you can come.

Fondly,
Christina

Spelling (p. 17)

Sample Answers:
1. (only)   I will tell you this only once.
2. (once)   Please tell me once more.
3. (name)   What is her name?
4. (cousin) We will meet your cousin then.
5. (picnic) I am going on a picnic.

Chapter One Review
Capitalizing (Names of Magazines) (p.18)

1. Alice and I enjoy reading <u>Reader's Digest</u> and <u>TV Guide</u>.
2. Frank and Ted read <u>Do It Yourself</u> and the <u>Complete Handyman</u>.
3. Chuck and I get <u>Sports Magazine</u> and the <u>Fisherman's Guide</u>.
4. Gale and Sally read romance magazines, such as <u>True Story</u>.
5. I like to read movie magazines, such as <u>Hollywood Magazine</u>.

Singular and Plural Subjects (p. 18)

You should have a line under the following.
1. Blanca Silva, friends (P)	4. it (S)
2. affairs (P)	5. I (S)
3. story (S)	

Recognizing Sentences (p. 18)

You should have a check by the following.
3. Stop running so fast.
4. Is that the truth?

Sentence Parts (p. 19)

You should have a line under the following.
1. When they go there.
3. After we saw them.
5. Until we arrive.
You should have a check by the following.
2. Help is on the way.
4. Anyone can do that.

Combining Sentences (p. 19)

1. The tall trees look like soldiers, and the flowers look like pretty young girls.
2. Hank was too tired to play, and his partner was not feeling well.
3. We studied hard for the test, and it was worth it.
4. George and Donna have a new home, and they just bought a new car and boat.
5. I would like to change jobs, and my boyfriend would like to move to another town.

Direct Quotations (p. 20)

1. Sidney said, "I need another helper."
2. Pina said, "That is not too strong."
3. Ali said, "I am visiting my family shortly."
4. Florence said, "My family is visiting me soon."
5. Teresa said, "These are enough supplies for the week."

End Marks (Punctuation Marks) (p. 20)

1. Where are we going?
2. Do you know the way?
3. This is the wrong road.
4. This is ridiculous!
5. Stop this minute.
   or: Stop this minute!

Adjectives and Linking Verbs (p. 20)

1. sadder
2. beautiful
3. better
4. cheerful
5. worst

Regular and Irregular Verbs (p. 21)

1. went; has gone
2. caught; has caught
3. forgot; has forgotten
4. ate; has eaten
5. tried; has tried

The Verb *Be* (p. 21)

1. has been
2. was
3. are
4. was
5. have been

The Verbs *Speak, Speaks, Spoke, Will Speak, Has Spoken, Have Spoken*, and *Had Spoken* (p. 21)

1. speaks
2. have spoken
3. will speak
4. spoken
5. spoke

The Words *A* and *An* (p. 21)

1. an orange
2. an oatmeal cracker
3. a closet
4. a boat
5. an ad
6. a show
7. a hole
8. a hammer
9. an ounce
10. an enemy

Writing an Invitation (p. 22)

Sample Letter:

> September 1, 1990
>
> Dear Ana,
>
> I am giving a party to celebrate my new job. The party is on Saturday, September 17, at 8:00 P.M. I'll have lots of food and drink. I hope you will come. Please phone by September 12 to tell me if you will.
>
> Fondly,
> Ricardo

Spelling (p. 22)

Sample Answers:
1. He is only here for a short time.
2. He has said that once too often.
3. I like my name.
4. My cousin is visiting me tomorrow.
5. We are all going on a picnic.

Chapter 2
Capitalizing (Names of Places) (p. 26)

1. Jim and Phyllis are traveling east.
2. Pauline and I are going to the East to see the Statue of Liberty.
3. The Franklin Bank is in North Carolina.
4. Ron traveled north, and then he went to the South.
5. Next May Mehdi and I are moving west to California.
6. Diego Juarez and his wife are going to the East soon.
7. Mrs. Peters lives in the East and travels south often.
8. The Russo family is going west to South Dakota.
9. Who was the president when the North and the South entered the Civil War?
10. In January we are going to the West and then to the North.

Combining Sentences (p. 27)

1. Jane is going to stop soon, but she has not finished yet.
2. I want to get married soon, but my girlfriend wants to wait.
3. We have a number of problems, but I feel we can work them out.
4. She wants to wait to have children, but I want them soon.
5. My sister thinks I won't marry Gloria, but my friends think I will.

Shortening Sentences (p. 28)

1. He has his coffee, toast, and cereal every morning.
2. I gave her my new dress, sweater, and pearls to wear.
3. My friends Bob, Gary, and Terry are coming to my house.
4. My old car, bike, and typewriter fell apart at the same time.
5. In the movie the wild foxes, wolves, and dogs ran together.

Sentence Parts (p. 29)

You should have a line under the following.
1. Although she is happy now
3. When she spoke
4. Until you decide
6. While we were there
9. Which one she liked

You should have a check by the following.
2. In a moment the game will be over.
5. Who is that person?
7. Help is on the way.
8. Run to the store for me.
10. Don't hold onto her.

Sentence Parts (Dependent and Independent Word Groups) (p. 30)

You should have underlined the following sentence parts.

1. <u>Although she was not feeling well</u>, she went to the party.
2. We were upset <u>when they showed it to us</u>.
3. <u>Before they saw us</u>, they were ready to leave.
4. We talked about our problems <u>while we were at Angela's house</u>.
5. <u>When you return</u>, we will go to the movies.
6. I wanted some praise <u>after I worked so hard</u>.
7. <u>Although he is nice</u>, I can't vote for him.
8. I will not change my mind <u>unless they change theirs</u>.
9. <u>Since it is too late to do anything now</u>, I will not go.
10. <u>Even though she is happy here</u>, she wants to quit.

Direct Quotations (p. 31)

1. Keung asked, "Who told you that lie?"
2. Hank asked, "What do you want?"
3. Marie said, "I need more time to think."
4. Kim said, "The car is not broken."
5. Carlos asked, "Will you come to see me soon?"
6. Tran asked, "Do you like little animals?"
7. Michel said, "I enjoy travelling."
8. Jerry asked, "Will I have time to do that?"
9. Hideo said, "There is nobody left who can do it."
10. Emilia said, "Let's have a party on New Year's Eve."

Direct and Indirect Quotations (pp. 32–33)

1. She said, "This is the happiest day of my life."
2. Mito said, "I want to visit you tomorrow."
3. Helen said, "I told Jack to buy the car."
4. Choi said, "I want to teach school next year."
5. Ted said, "I am going on vacation tomorrow."
6. Flores said, "The mail has not arrived yet."
7. She said, "I do not need any help."
8. Dick said, "The car door is stuck."
9. Betty said, "My boss is giving me a raise."
10. Henry said, "I will ask my boss for a raise."

Pronouns (p. 34)

1. She; me
2. I; them
3. We; them
4. They; us
5. They; us
6. It; us
7. We; it
8. She; us
9. I; them
10. she; us

More Than One (Plural) (p. 35)

1. cars
2. elves
3. lashes
4. women
5. mice
6. crashes
7. Charleses
8. kisses
9. flies
10. lunches
11. wives
12. foxes
13. faces
14. teeth
15. beds
16. messes
17. witches
18. candies
19. days
20. babies

The Verbs *Steal, Steals, Stole, Will Steal, Has Stolen, Have Stolen,* and *Had Stolen* (p. 36)

1. stolen
2. stolen
3. stole
4. stolen
5. stole
6. stole
7. steal
8. stolen
9. stolen
10. steal

Adverbs (p. 37)

1. better
2. best
3. heaviest
4. more rapidly
5. more slowly
6. hardest
7. faster
8. tightest
9. more often **or** oftener
10. louder

Showing Ownership or Belonging To (Possession) (p. 38)

1. goose's
2. woman's
3. wives'
4. game's
5. couch's
6. shelves'
7. candy's
8. task's
9. hostess's
10. tomato's

Contractions (p. 39)

1. she's
2. we've
3. I've
4. they've
5. you're
6. we're
7. I'm
8. they're
9. she's
10. it's

Spelling (p. 40)

Sample Answers:
1. (good-bye) James said, "Good-bye, I'll see you later."
2. (again) Let's do it again.
3. (week) I'll see you in a week.
4. (color) Color this green.
5. (blue) Blue is her favorite color.

Chapter Two Review

Capitalizing (Names of Places) (p. 41)

1. Aunt Lisa and I live in North Dakota and like to travel east.
2. Jim, Ted, and José are going to the South on vacation.
3. My Uncle Mike has traveled to the West and all over.
4. Our club is taking a bus trip to the East this summer.
5. I live in West Virginia and travel to South Carolina often.

Combining Sentences (pp. 41–42)

1. Marriage is a big step, but I am ready for it.
2. My boyfriend wants us to live together first, but my parents are very upset about this.
3. They do not want me to move in with my boyfriend, but I do not want to lose him.
4. I really want to get married and raise a family, but I can't convince my boyfriend to do this.
5. I may move in with my boyfriend, but it's not what I really want to do.

Shortening Sentences (p. 42)

1. My friends Mary, Kim, and Sue are here.
2. The hot roll, bacon, and eggs are delicious.
3. My pals Jack, Herbert, Artie, Julio, and I are going hunting next week.
4. Kenji's old couch, chair, and table need to be repaired.
5. I love my dog, cat, and pet canary.

Sentence Parts (p. 42)

You should have a line under the following.
1. When Jane leaves
2. Until I can be on my own
4. After the game is over
You should have a check by each of the following.
3. Please go there with me.
5. This is very funny.

Sentence Parts (Independent and Dependent Word Groups) (p. 43)

You should have underlined the following parts of the sentences.
1. When Doris came to the party, she looked very upset.
2. She left suddenly after she had been there a short while.
3. While we were talking about this, we heard some noise outside.
4. We didn't pay too much attention to it since it was very noisy inside.
5. When we left, we saw Doris lying face down in the street.

Direct Quotations (p. 43)

1. Julio said, "This year is going to be our best one."
2. Peter asked, "Who could be so stupid?"
3. George asked, "Why are they talking so long?"
4. Martin said, "I refuse to pay so much for this."
5. Yuriko said, "That man just stole something from the store."

Direct and Indirect Quotations (p. 43)

1. Gloria said, "The roads are very slippery today."
2. Sally said, "The bus is running late today."
3. Antoine said, "My car has a flat tire."
4. Paul said, "I need a ride home from work."
5. Maria said, "I have more work to do."

Pronouns (p. 44)

1. I; him
2. I; them
3. She; him
4. They; us
5. We; him

More than One (Plural) (p. 44)

1. tires
2. bodies
3. boxes
4. scarves
5. wives
6. children
7. knives
8. wolves
9. roofs
10. buildings

The Verbs *Steal, Steals, Stole, Will Steal, Has Stolen, Have Stolen*, and *Had Stolen* (p. 44)

1. stole
2. stolen
3. will steal **or** steal
4. stolen
5. steals

Adverbs (p. 44)

1. hardest
2. more poorly
3. harder
4. most carelessly
5. more friendly **or** friendlier

Showing Ownership or Belonging To (Possession) (p. 45)

1. wolf's
2. ladies'
3. tool's
4. James's
5. children's
6. toy's
7. sales'
8. box's
9. fire's
10. men's

Contractions (p. 45)

1. I've
2. they've
3. he's
4. they're
5. it's
6. we're
7. she's
8. you're
9. it's
10. you've

Spelling (p. 45)

Sample Answers:
1. It is hard saying good-bye to someone you love.
2. Do we have to do this again?
3. This is the third week we have done this.
4. Red is my favorite color.
5. Judy's favorite color is blue.

Chapter 3

Capitalizing (Common Nouns and Proper Nouns) (p. 48)

1. Mexico
2. James
3. C
4. ABC Company
5. C
6. Tuesday
7. Chicago
8. C
9. Columbus Day
10. Father's Day
11. C
12. C
13. Carol
14. Ohio
15. C
16. year
17. World War II
18. Italy
19. Jeff
20. Judge Brown

Combining Sentences (pp. 49–50)

1. My brother fell in love with a beautiful girl, but she does not love him.
2. He walks around with a long face all the time, and it is difficult to cheer him up.
3. I am trying to get them together, but it is probably a lost cause.
4. My brother needs to meet someone else, or he will become even more depressed.
5. We have to do something soon, or my brother will wind up in the hospital.

Combining Sentences (pp. 51–52)

1. Go to the doctor today for a check-up, or you may have a problem later on.
2. Gregory needs to see a lawyer, and you also need advice.
3. This may work fine, but I am not too sure.
4. Mr. and Mrs. Knott are checking out today, but their friends are staying another day.
5. Do you want to stay here another day, or do we need to go home?

Sentence Parts (Independent and Dependent Word Groups) (p. 53)

You should have a line under the following.
1. They should not go there when it is dark.
2. Although I like my work, I don't want to do anything now.
3. After we saw them, we knew they were in trouble.
4. I was very tired after I worked so hard.
5. Even though she practices hard, she doesn't play too well.
6. When the storm started, we were on the road.
7. I am going there because I love him.
8. Sara will meet you there unless she changes her mind.
9. Come back to my house when the show is over.
10. Unless you want trouble, try to help them.

Combining Independent and Dependent Word Groups (p. 54)

1. e Herb found his door open when he came home.
2. a Sharon went to the game because she loves football.
3. g It is no fun to go out if you have no pals.
4. f We are waiting until Hossein arrives.
5. h I hold that against her because she hurt my friend.
6. j The police arrived at my home after the crook had left.
7. b Giorgio practices the piano every day until his fingers are tired.
8. c My car will not move because it is out of gas.
9. d Matsue and Junko have done a lot since they left school.
10. i The ballplayers are not happy because they lost the game.

The Pronouns *Anybody, Anyone, Everybody, Everyone, Nobody, No One, Somebody,* and *Someone* (p. 55)

You should have a line under the following.
1. is
2. Has
3. has
4. does
5. knows
6. helps
7. was
8. reads
9. has
10. works

The Verbs *Write, Writes, Wrote, Will Write, Has Written, Have Written,* and *Had Written* (p. 56)

1. wrote
2. write
3. written
4. writes **or** will write
5. written
6. wrote
7. written
8. wrote
9. written
10. will write

Showing Ownership or Belonging To (Possession) (p. 57)

1. car's
2. Jennifer's
3. geese's
4. wife's
5. thief's
6. owner's
7. children's
8. Victor's
9. Giselle's
10. church's

The Comma (Setting Off Words) (p. 58)

1. Moreover, I have a lot of time to do it.
2. Indeed, that is a good idea.
3. She said, however, that she would stay with us.
4. We felt, moreover, that we could make a lot of money that way.
5. She saw, however, that it wouldn't work.
6. Therefore, I need more time to stay here.
7. He does look silly, indeed.
8. Furthermore, anyone who says anything will be in trouble.
9. We learned, for example, that it would be dangerous to do that.
10. You can, perhaps, think of another way to do it.

Abbreviations (Shortened Words) (p. 59)

1. Blvd.
2. A.M.
3. Co.
4. Rev.; St.
5. P.M.
6. Rev.
7. Dr.; Co.
8. Dr.; Ave.
9. Co.
10. Dr.

Writing a Business Letter (pp. 60–61)

Sample Letter:

> 74 Sixth Ave.
> New York, New York 10022
> December 4, 1990
>
> President
> XYZ Tool Co.
> 791 Moore St.
> New York, New York 10003
>
> Dear Sir or Madam:
>
> I ordered tool set #231 from your company and received set #234 instead. I sent back the wrong set but never received the set I ordered. This has been going on for six weeks. I am very upset about this. You have my money, but I do not have my tools. This is certainly no way to do business.
>
> Yours truly,
> Henry Jones

Spelling (p. 62)

Sample Answers:
1. (since) Since yesterday, I have felt better.
2. (receive) I did not receive my package.
3. (because) I will go away with you because I love you.
4. (cough) I seem to have a cough.
5. (piece) I'd like a piece of cake.

Alphabetizing (Using the Dictionary) (p. 63)

1. No
2. Yes
3. No
4. No
5. No
6. No
7. No
8. No
9. No
10. Yes

Chapter Three Review

Capitalizing (Common Nouns and Proper Nouns) (p. 64)

1. North Carolina
2. Miss Brown
3. holiday
4. C
5. Stone Company
6. New Mexico
7. C
8. Mother's Day
9. Robert
10. France

Combining Sentences (pp. 64–65)

1. You should help your parents more, and your brother should try to be nicer to them.
2. The phone rang, but there was no one on the line.
3. The workers want a raise, but they do not want to strike.
4. The workers need more money, but their company can't afford to give raises.
5. Jack must fly to Chicago today, or he will lose his plane fare.

Sentence Parts (Independent and Dependent Word Groups) (p. 65)

You should have a line under the following.
1. After I left, someone robbed the store.
2. I am leaving when she arrives.
3. Unless you hear differently, I will meet you later.
4. I will help her because she needs my help.
5. I get a headache when she is here.

Combining Independent and Dependent Word Groups (p. 65)

1. e Sue wants to be a designer because she loves art.
2. a Art was her best subject when she was in school.
3. d Sue and her sister are going into business after they save enough money.
4. b Their brother is helping them raise money because he believes in them.
5. c Their parents are helping until they can be on their own.

The Pronouns *Anybody, Anyone, Everybody, Everyone, Nobody, No One, Somebody,* and *Someone* (p. 65)

You should have underlined the following.
1. wants
2. seems
3. has
4. is
5. Does

The Verbs *Write, Writes, Wrote, Will Write, Has Written, Have Written,* and *Had Written* (p. 66)

1. wrote
2. write
3. written
4. will write
5. written

Showing Ownership or Belonging To (Possession) (p. 66)

1. Raul's
2. Alice's
3. car's
4. wives'
5. roses'

The Comma (Setting off Words) (p. 66)

1. Therefore, I do not need to go.
2. Patricio said, moreover, that he would do it.
3. It is too dangerous, however.
4. We should, perhaps, put it off.
5. Frank and Mike, however, want to do it now.

Abbreviations (Shortened Words) (pp. 66–67)

1. Rev.; Ave.
2. Dr.; St.
3. Co.; Dr.
4. Rev. P.M.
5. Co.; Rd.

Writing a Business Letter (p. 67)

Sample Letter:

> 91 Ford Avenue
> Philadelphia, Pennsylvania 19117
> February 11, 1990
>
> President
> Empire Clothing Company
> 368 Field Avenue
> Tulsa, Oklahoma 74121
>
> Dear Sir or Madam:
>
> I ordered a jacket (#1425) from your catalog two months ago. Four weeks ago, I received a jacket, but it was not the one I ordered. I sent back the jacket. Since then I have not heard anything from your company. I would like either the jacket I ordered or my money back.
>
> Sincerely yours,
> Robert Burns

Spelling (p. 68)

Sample Answers:
1. I haven't seen them since last week.
2. Did you receive my letter?
3. Because I love you, I need you.
4. That is a bad cough.
5. Which piece do you want?

Alphabetizing (Using the Dictionary) (p. 68)

1. Yes
2. Yes
3. No
4. No
5. Yes

Chapter 4

Capitalizing (Historical Periods and Documents) (pp. 72–73)

1. The American Constitution is a very special document.
2. The American Revolution had several causes.
3. The Russian Revolution took place after the American Revolution.
4. The French Revolution took place after the American Revolution.
5. The Bill of Rights is part of the Constitution.
6. In Pauline's history class she learned about the Roman Empire.
7. The Industrial Age in the United States saw the rise of cities.
8. In Washington, D.C., I visited the Lincoln Memorial.
9. On Veteran's Day we honor those who fought for our country.
10. Next March Nina and I are visiting Philadelphia to see the Liberty Bell.

Combining Sentences (pp. 74–75)

1. This is a terrible story, butit must be told.
2. Jeff is a married man, but he goes out with women.
3. One woman he went out with had AIDS, and she gave the virus to Jeff.
4. Jeff did not know he had the virus, or he would have avoided giving it to his wife.
5. His wife was expecting a baby, and the baby was born with AIDS.

Sentence Parts (Independent and Dependent Word Groups) (p. 76)

You should have a line under the following.
1. <u>Although he feels sorry about it,</u> it is too late.
2. People must be more careful <u>because there are more dangers today.</u>
3. <u>Unless people protect themselves properly,</u> they may have big problems.
4. Unfortunately, little children get hurt <u>because some adults are careless.</u>
5. It is very sad <u>when a baby is born with AIDS.</u>
6. It is something <u>that should not have happened.</u>
7. <u>After people heard about it,</u> they avoided him.
8. Now, his friends cross the street <u>when they see him.</u>
9. His poor wife cries <u>when she visits her baby in the hospital.</u>
10. This is a terrible tragedy <u>because a whole family has been destroyed.</u>

End Marks (Punctuation Marks) (p. 77)

1. Ben asked when they were leaving.
2. Andres asked who was meeting them later.
3. What kind of person would do that?
4. Is she really that angry at us?
5. Francis asked why they did that.
6. Marianne asked how old she was.
7. Did the police arrest anyone?
8. What is her address?
9. Nader asked whether the mail was due shortly.
10. Everyone wondered what caused the accident.

Pronouns (Showing Ownership or Belonging To) (pp. 78–79)

1. his
2. hers; her
3. his; his
4. theirs; their
5. Her
6. His **or** Her
7. his
8. his
9. his
10. its

The Pronouns *Who, Whom,* and *Whose* (p. 80)

1. whom
2. Whose
3. Who
4. whom
5. Who
6. whom
7. Who
8. Whose
9. Whose
10. Who

The Verbs *Lay, Lays, Laid, Will Lay, Has Laid, Have Laid,* and *Had Laid* (p. 81)

1. Lay	5. lays	8. laid
2. lay	6. laid	9. laid
3. laid	7. laid	10. laid
4. laid		

Contractions (p. 82)

1. he'll	8. wasn't	15. we'll
2. it'll	9. aren't	16. haven't
3. shouldn't	10. hadn't	17. isn't
4. won't	11. didn't	18. weren't
5. they'll	12. couldn't	19. wouldn't
6. don't	13. can't	20. she'll
7. hasn't	14. I'll	

Writing the Time of Day (p. 83)

1. 2:10 P.M.	5. 2:15 A.M.	8. 3:45 P.M.
2. 12:05 P.M.	6. 1:05 A.M.	9. 7:14 A.M.
3. 3:25 A.M.	7. 9:12 A.M.	10. 9:05 P.M.
4. 10:15 A.M.		

Writing Paragraphs (p. 84)

You should have underlined the following words in the paragraph.

Maxine needs help. <u>Unfortunately</u>, she does not admit it. <u>Before</u>, Maxine used to wonder aloud whether she was drinking too much. <u>Now</u>, even though she drinks more, she thinks she drinks moderately. <u>Finally</u>, either Maxine will stop denying her alcoholism, or drink will rule her life until she dies.

Organizing Sentences into a Paragraph (pp. 85–86)

You should have written the following.

Betty and Jane are identical twins. However, they were raised in separate families and never saw each other until last week. Nevertheless, there are amazing similarities between them. For example, both of them are hairdressers. In addition, they are both talented at dancing, drawing, and guitar playing. Now they are eager to find out in what other ways they are similar.

Proofreading (p. 87)

This is the paragraph as you should have written it. The words that were changed are underlined.

<u>Our</u> writing <u>assignments</u> are never very <u>interesting</u>. <u>For</u> example, at the <u>beginning</u> of the term, we <u>wrote</u> about what we wanted to get out of the class. <u>Later</u>, we wrote about <u>different</u> <u>holidays</u>. <u>Sometimes</u> we write about the <u>weather</u> or members of our <u>families</u>. I would like to <u>write</u> about <u>something</u> more <u>exciting</u>.

Spelling (p. 88)

Sample Answers:

1. (health)	His health is not very good.
2. (shoes)	I hate to buy shoes.
3. (sometimes)	Sometimes I like to be by myself.
4. (ache)	Hank has an ache in his leg.
5. (straight)	Can you walk a straight line?

Chapter Four Review

Capitalizing (Historical Periods and Documents) (p. 89)

1. The Industrial Revolution began in England over two hundred years ago.
2. We are living in the Computer Age
3. A new system of government was set up by the American Constitution.
4. The American Revolution was different from the French Revolution and the Russian Revolution.
5. The Bill of Rights protects the rights of each of us.

Combining Sentences (pp. 89–90)

1. Juana would like to go with you, but she has to go the dentist.
2. It has been raining for ten days, but there haven't been any floods.
3. We helped them yesterday, and they helped us today.
4. I borrowed my friend's car for a quick run to the store, but it ran out of gas on the way.
5. Do your work on time, or it will just become too much for you.

Sentence Parts (Independent and Dependent Word Groups) (p. 90)

You should have a line under the following.
1. We often get up late <u>when we are on vacation.</u>
2. <u>After we had eaten so much,</u> we didn't want to go.
3. No one called the hotel <u>where they are staying.</u>
4. Several people saw them yesterday <u>while they were here</u>.
5. <u>Although it is very late</u>, I am still going.

End Marks (Punctuation Marks) (p. 90)

1. Sheila asked when she wanted to go.
2. George asked when she was going to the store.
3. Nobody wanted to ask why no one called the police.
4. When did she arrive here?
5. Harry asked who the woman was.

Pronouns (Showing Ownership or Belonging To) (p. 91)

1. hers; her	3. his; his	5. Its
2. mine	4. Their	

The Pronouns *Who*, *Whom*, and *Whose* (p. 91)

1. whom	3. Who	5. whom
2. Whose	4. Who	

The Verbs *Lay, Lays, Laid, Will Lay, Has Laid, Have Laid,* and *Had Laid* (p. 91)

1. laid	3. will lay	5. lay
2. lays	4. laid	

Contractions (p. 92)

1. I'll	5. doesn't	8. wouldn't
2. they'll	6. you'll	9. haven't
3. shouldn't	7. she'll	10. don't
4. hasn't		

Writing the Time of Day (p. 92)

1. 2:05 A.M.	3. 8:10 A.M.	5. 5:25 A.M.
2. 12:05 P.M.	4. 10:10 P.M.	

Writing Paragraphs (p. 92)

You should have underlined the following words in the paragraph.

The blood supply was running low, so an appeal went to the public to give blood. <u>However</u>, there was almost no increase in the rate of blood donations after the appeal. People were afraid that giving blood might put them at risk for AIDS. <u>Of course</u>, giving blood does not put people at risk. <u>In fact</u>, receiving blood is not as risky now as it was a few years ago.

Organizing Sentences into a Paragraph (pp. 92–93)

Mrs. Tanaka has developed a thriving babysitting service. The idea for the service began to come to her when she got more requests to babysit than she could handle. In the beginning, she recommended babysitters she knew. Later, for a small fee, she lined up babysitters for parents who needed them. Because she always recommends dependable sitters, her service has become very popular. As a result, she is so busy filling requests for sitters that she has no time to babysit anymore.

Proofreading (p. 93)

This is the paragraph as you should have written it. The parts that were changed are underlined.

<u>I</u> <u>answered</u> an ad in the <u>New York Times</u> for a job <u>recently</u>. <u>Someone</u> called me from the <u>Acme</u> <u>Plumbing</u> <u>Co</u>. <u>I</u> was very <u>nervous</u> while <u>I</u> was being interviewed<u>,</u> and <u>I</u> could <u>hardly</u> talk. Needless to say<u>,</u> <u>I</u> <u>didn't</u> get the job<u>.</u> I need to <u>practice</u> going on interviews.

Spelling (p. 93)

Sample Answers:
1. Exercise and good diet are important for health.
2. I buy shoes for comfort as well as for style.
3. Sometimes I feel happy for no reason.
4. I had an ache in my wrist.
5. I went straight home.

Chapter 5

Capitalizing (pp. 96–97)

1. I am going west in the spring to visit my Aunt Kiyo.
2. Jim and I are taking Spanish and French in the fall.
3. During the football season, I am going to visit my cousin.
4. Mei plays checkers and chess in the fall.
5. My Uncle Joe and his daughter love to play tennis.
6. My aunt says that spring is my Uncle Julio's favorite season.
7. On Sunday our club is having a picnic in the western part of town.
8. I need help in English, Spanish, and geography.
9. Football and basketball are my cousin's favorite sports.
10. Last spring we traveled east, and I met a famous actor.

Word Order in Sentences (p. 98)

1. My sister, brother, and wife get along well together.
2. The terrible fight at my office frightened us.
3. We were shocked when the two men started to hit each other.
4. Our office looked like it had been hit by a storm.
5. When the police arrived, the fight was still going on. **or**: The fight was still going on when the police arrived.

Pronouns and What They Refer to (p. 99)

1. his **or** my	5. his **or** her	8. their
2. his	6. its	9. her
3. their	7. their	10. our
4. its		

The Verbs *Lie, Lies, Lay, Will Lie, Has Lain, Have Lain,* and *Had Lain* (p. 100)

1. lie	5. lain	8. lies
2. lay	6. will lie	9. lain
3. will lie	7. lain	10. lies
4. lain		

The Verbs *Teach* and *Learn* (p. 101)

1. taught	5. teach	8. taught
2. learned	6. learned	9. teaches
3. teach	7. have learned	10. learn
4. learn		

The Words *Its* and *It's*, *Their* and *They're*, and *Whose* and *Who's* (p. 102)

1. It's	5. They're	8. Whose
2. Whose	6. Whose	9. It's
3. Who's	7. They're	10. it's
4. their		

The Comma (p. 103)

1. NC
2. NC
3. It has been a long, hard year.
4. The handsome, kind boy is here.
5. NC
6. My itchy, rough sweater is gone.
7. The frightened, hurt man thanked us for our help.
8. NC
9. We looked through the frosty, cold window.
10. NC

Organizing Sentences into a Paragraph (pp. 104–105)

You should have written the following.

David applied for a job with the police and was scheduled to take the physical strength test on Wednesday. Fortunately, he was athletic and would pass easily. However, the day before, he broke his foot. Therefore, he had to reschedule his test. Unfortunately, no appointments were available for at least six months. David had no choice but to wait.

Sentence Variety (p. 106)

Sample Paragraph:

My oldest brother is always in trouble with the law and is now in a detention center. Our parents could not control him, and marriage has not helped him mature. My sisters, my other brothers, and I are afraid of him. We wish we could find the thing to do that would make him straighten out.

Sentence Variety (p. 107)

Sample Paragraph:

The man was on the run. He wore a hat that covered his eyes, a dark coat with the collar turned up, and dark glasses. Carrying an old, torn bag, he walked swiftly. He kept one hand in his pocket and kept looking over his shoulder. When he heard a noise, he hid in the shadows of the night.

Proofreading (p. 108)

This is the paragraph as you should have written it. The words that were changed are underlined.

Most Pilgrim children's lives in school weren't very easy. They usually had strict teachers. When children talked in school, they were punished. Often they were whipped. The children were afraid of the teachers. They didn't like school, and they were glad when the day was over.

Spelling (p. 109)

Sample Answers:
1. (develop)   Please develop these films for me.
2. (judgment)   Don't make a judgment until you have all the facts.
3. (instead)   Let's go there instead.
4. (just)   I want to see her for just a moment.
5. (lose)   How could we lose the game to them?

Alphabetizing (Using the Phone Book) (p. 110)

1. Yes	3. Yes	5. Yes	7. No	9. No
2. Yes	4. No	6. Yes	8. No	10. Yes

Chapter Five Review

Capitalizing (p. 111)

1. In the fall, Florence and I are going to the North to visit our cousins.
2. My Italian cousin and my Irish cousin are going to Ireland and Italy next spring.
3. Lan and Jim live on Kean Road and work with computers.
4. My mother and Aunt Joan went east to visit the Statue of Liberty.
5. My favorite season is the summer, and my favorite day is Saturday.

Word Order in Sentences (pp. 111–112)

1. Gil, Luz, Tanako, and I work in a hospital on Northern Boulevard.
2. In the past year there have been a great number of odd deaths.
   or: There have been a great number of odd deaths in the past year.
3. Many elderly patients were injected with a deadly poison.
4. One nurse had taken care of all the patients before they died.
5. The nurses, doctors, and police knew who the murderer was.

Pronouns and What They Refer To (p. 112)

1. his	3. my	5. its
2. their	4. her	

The Verbs *Lie, Lies, Lay, Will Lie, Has Lain, Have Lain,* and *Had Lain* (p. 112)

1. lain	3. lies	5. Lie
2. lay	4. will lie	

The Verbs *Teach* and *Learn* (p. 112)

1. taught	3. learned	5. will teach
2. has taught	4. learn	

The Words *Its* and *It's*, *Their* and *They're*, and *Whose* and *Who's* (p. 113)

1. Whose
2. Who's
3. They're
4. It's
5. its

The Comma (p. 113)

1. NC
2. The ugly, bare room needs decorating.
3. The slender, curly-haired woman laughed loudly.
4. NC
5. The lost, scared girl stared blindly at us.

Organizing Sentences into a Paragraph (p. 113)

You should have written the following.

Mike had a nerve-wracking day ahead of him, and he didn't want to get up. He lay in bed until his wife said that things would work out, no matter what happened. That helped him gather the courage to get ready for work. While he was eating breakfast, he thought about all the bills that had to be paid and the other constant expenses. Finally, he was ready to go, but he wasn't prepared to find out whether he was one of the two hundred to be laid off today.

Sentence Variety (p. 114)

Sample Paragraphs:

I am thirty-five years old, and I still live at home with my parents and sister. I still have the same room I had when I was a child, and I still do the same things. My chances of meeting someone and getting married are not very good. In addition, the older I get, the more unhappy I get.

I need to get my own apartment, but my parents get upset when I talk about this. They think I am still a child and treat me that way. Obviously, there must be something wrong with me. I have an excellent job, earn good money, and want to be independent, but I am afraid to leave home.

Proofreading (p. 115)

This is the paragraph as you should have written it. The words that were changed are underlined.

Have you ever seen an empty house and wondered who had lived there ? Whenever I would have to walk past a certain house in my neighborhood, I would cross the street and walk on the other side. The house has been boarded up for as long as I can remember. Everyone talks about the house in hushed voices. Some say Dracula lived there. Frankly, I don't take any chances. I just don't walk past the house.

Spelling (p. 115)

Sample Answers:
1. He will develop into a fine young man.
2. That judgment sounds rather harsh.
3. Instead of eating home, let's have a picnic.
4. Please wait for just one minute.
5. Did you lose the game?

Alphabetizing (Using the Phone Book) (p. 116)

1. No   2. No   3. Yes   4. No   5. Yes

Posttest

Capitalizing (p. 118)

1. Spanish
2. winter
3. South Carolina
4. Rev. James Corbett
5. south
6. island
7. C
8. grammar
9. place
10. mother

Singular and Plural Subjects (p. 118)

You should have a line under the following.
1. relatives (P)
2. Everybody (S)
3. Nobody (S)
4. meeting (S)
5. Anyone (S)

Recognizing Sentences (p. 118)

You should have a check by each of the following.
1. Talk more softly.
5. Are you certain about this?

Word Order in Sentences (p. 119)

1. Ken, Manuel, Koyi, and I went on a hunting trip together.
2. We brought lots of sandwiches, salads, snacks, and drinks with us.
3. When we got to the hunting grounds, we unpacked our gear.
   or: We unpacked our gear when we got to the hunting grounds.
4. First, we set up our tents, and then we sat down to rest.
5. Suddenly, we saw three deer run right past us.

Combining Sentences (pp. 119–120)

1. My friend José left his country, and he came to the United States of America.
2. He had to come to this country, or his enemies would have killed him.
3. José is an illegal alien, and he does not have a job.
4. He is learning English, but no one will hire him.
5. José is not happy here, but it is too dangerous for him to return to his country.

Shortening Sentences (p. 120)

1. Her friends Pedro, Leonardo, David, and Raul have their own band.
2. The mayor asked the police, fire fighters, transit workers, and sanitation workers to a party.
3. Elena, Fabio, Harue, and I are studying for English tests.
4. I listen to the radio, read papers, and watch television a lot.
5. Peter likes funny movies, stories, and jokes.

Sentence Parts (p. 120)

You should have a line under the following.
1. When he does such things.
3. Who the man is.
4. Until I can see him.

You should have a check by the following.
2. Who knows her?
5. How well do you know him?

Sentence Parts (Independent and Dependent Word Groups) (p. 121)

You should have underlined the following parts of the sentences.
1. Aliens can become citizens if they have been here a certain number of years.
2. Unless they learn English, they will have problems here.
3. Many aliens are becoming citizens after they learn English.
4. It is difficult for some aliens because people take advantage of them.
5. Many aliens have high hopes when they come here.

Direct Quotations (p. 121)

1. Gary said, "That does not belong here."
2. Christine asked, "Why aren't you doing your work?"
3. Robert said, "The computer is not working properly."
4. Arthur asked, "Are you interested in some good advice?"
5. Terry asked, "Will this make a lot of money?"

Direct and Indirect Quotations (pp. 121–122)

1. Adela said, "I love my new house."
2. Mr. Petridis said, "I want my people to work harder."
3. Miss Vega said, "I need to study this some more."
4. I said, "I do not have any time for that."
5. Hiroshi said, "I am very lucky to have such a good job."

End Marks (Punctuation Marks) (p. 122)

1. He asked whether we had a chance.
2. They said that we didn't.
3. Why don't we have a chance?
4. The manager asked why we were interested in trying out.
5. We asked why he had to know.

Pronouns (p. 122)

1. He, me
2. They, us
3. He, her
4. She, him
5. We, them

Pronouns and What They Refer To (p. 122)

1. his
2. their
3. her
4. his
5. my

Pronouns (Showing Ownership or Belonging To (p. 123)

1. mine
2. his
3. her
4. Their
5. its

The Pronouns *Anybody, Anyone, Everybody, Everyone, Nobody, No One, Somebody,* and *Someone* (p. 123)

You should have a line under the following.
1. seems
2. belongs
3. is
4. knows
5. has

The Words *Who, Whom,* and *Whose* (p. 123)

1. Whose
2. Who
3. Who
4. whom
5. whom

More Than One (Plural) (p. 124)

1. dishes
2. rocks
3. teeth
4. taxes
5. spies
6. shelves
7. deer
8. stitches
9. lunches
10. calves

Adjectives and Linking Verbs (p. 124)

1. sour
2. loud
3. delicious
4. well
5. prettier

Regular and Irregular Verbs (p. 124)

1. looked, has looked
2. learned, has learned
3. tried, has tried
4. planted, has planted
5. lay, has lain
6. taught, has taught
7. wrote, has written
8. went, has gone
9. laid, has laid
10. stole, has stolen

The Verb *Be* (p. 125)

1. has been
2. is
3. was
4. has been
5. were

The Verbs *Speak, Speaks, Spoke, Will Speak, Has Spoken, Have Spoken,* and *Had Spoken* (p. 125)

1. spoke 3. speaks 5. spoke
2. will speak 4. spoken

The Verbs *Steal, Steals, Stole, Will Steal, Has Stolen, Have Stolen,* and *Had Stolen* (p. 125)

1. stole 3. stolen 5. stolen
2. steals 4. will steal

The Verbs *Write, Writes, Wrote, Will Write, Has Written, Have Written,* and *Had Written* (p. 125)

1. write 3. will write 5. written
2. wrote 4. written

The Verbs *Lay, Lays, Laid, Will Lay, Has Laid, Have Laid,* and *Had Laid* (p. 126)

1. laid 3. lays 5. Lay
2. laid 4. will lay

The Verbs *Lie, Lies, Lay, Will Lie, Has Lain, Have Lain, Had Lain* (p. 126)

1. will lie 3. lies 5. lay
2. lain 4. Lie

The Verbs *Teach* and *Learn* (p. 126)

1. learns 3. learned 5. learned
2. teaches 4. taught

Adverbs (p. 126)

1. more highly 3. most fiercely 5. fastest
2. more clearly 4. best

Showing Ownership or Belonging To (Possession) (p. 127)

1. child's 3. James's 5. watch's
2. deer's 4. spy's

The Words *Its* and *It's, Their* and *They're,* and *Whose* and *Who's* (p. 127)

1. Its 3. Who's 5. They're
2. Whose 4. Their

The Comma (p. 127)

1. Of course, I'm buying that new white car.
2. Indeed, it is a nice, friendly little kitten.
3. This has been a long, hard year.
4. NC
5. Certainly, this is good, sturdy furniture.

Abbreviations (Shortened Words) (pp. 127–128)

1. Rev.; Ave.; Co. 4. A.M.; Dr.; St.
2. Dr.; Rd.; A.M. 5. Co.; Blvd.
3. Rev.; Dr.

Contractions (p. 128)

1. I've 5. it's 8. can't
2. she's 6. you'll 9. we're
3. doesn't 7. wouldn't 10. it'll
4. won't

Writing the Time of Day (p. 128)

1. 5:25 P.M. 5. 7:30 P.M. 8. 7:25 A.M.
2. 1:05 A.M. 6. 10:45 P.M. 9. 4:15 P.M.
3. 3:30 P.M. 7. 6:15 P.M. 10. 8:50 A.M.
4. 11:10 A.M.

The Words *A* and *An* (p. 128)

1. an apron 6. a union card
2. an unbuilt house 7. a helper
3. an ice bag 8. an unkind man
4. a hug 9. an illegal alien
5. an agreement 10. a hill

Writing Paragraphs (p. 129)

You should have underlined the following words.

Rosa has been unhappily married for thirty years. In spite of her unhappiness, Rosa has never considered divorce. It would be unthinkable, especially since she is a mother and a grandmother. Moreover, if she had considered it, she would have been the first woman in her family to have done so. Therefore, since Rosa feels about divorce as she does, she may go to the grave an unhappy wife.

Organizing Sentences into a Paragraph (p. 129)

You should have the following:

Not long after her last daughter moved out, Rosa felt as though she could not stand living in the same house alone with her husband for another minute. At the same time, she began to wonder what it would be like if she just left. Immediately, she realized that she did not want to live with any of her children. In addition, she became aware that she might have trouble supporting herself. After a few minutes of such thoughts, Rosa put on her apron, sighed, and set the table for two.

Sentence Variety (p. 130)

Sample Paragraph:

    A nervous man entered the diner and looked around angrily. He was wearing a suit that was a bit large for him, and he looked evil. The people having their supper in the diner began to feel uncomfortable. Before the man walked in, they had been talking about the jail break. All day newscasters kept saying that the escaped convict was armed and dangerous. The rising tension in the diner made everyone nervous. Something was going to happen.

Proofreading (p. 130)

This is the paragraph as you should have written it. The words that were changed are underlined.

    I met an incredible person the other day. He came here from El Salvador a number of years ago. He worked hard and earned enough money to bring his family here. Today he has his own business, his own car, and his own home. Now he helps other people who come here from his country. Everybody loves him.

Writing an Invitation (p. 131)

Sample Letter:

June 12, 1990

Dear Daris and Chepa,

    We are having a party to celebrate John's graduation from high school and would love you to join us. The party is on Sunday, June 28, at 2:30 P.M. at our home. Everyone will be here.

    Please phone by June 22 to let us know if you will be coming. Our number is 555-8765

Best wishes,
Mary and George Davis

Writing a Business Letter (p. 132)

Sample Letter:

321 Brook Avenue
Chicago, Illinois 60612
November 12, 1990

President
Hoover's Department Store
211 Main Boulevard
Chicago, Illinois 60606

Dear Sir or Madam:

    I ordered a pair of boots from you at the end of September after I saw them advertised in the *Chicago Globe*. I received the boots right away. However, they were the wrong boots.

    I phoned your store and was told that I should bring them back. I did, but you did not have the ones I ordered in stock. I was promised that I would receive the correct boots soon. It is now two months later, and I still do not have my boots. I am very annoyed about this. If I do not get the boots within a week, I want my money back.

Sincerely,
John Murphy

Spelling (p. 133)

1. picnic
2. name
3. good-bye
4. health
5. instead
6. because
7. ache
8. straight
9. cough
10. shoes
11. cousin
12. only
13. again
14. just
15. judgment
16. sometimes
17. since
18. color
19. receive
20. develop

Alphabetizing (Using the Phone Book) (p. 133)

1. Yes   2. No   3. Yes   4. Yes   5. Yes